RAFAIL KOSOVSKY

1307 DAYS UNDER THE
NOOSE

LOS ANGELES

2008

ISBN: 978-0-6152-4113-5

Publisher: Rafail Kosovsky

In loving memory of my two twelve-year-old sisters Fanya and Nura, murdered by Nazis in the Black Forest near the village of Chervonoe, Ukraine, in September, 1941

TABLE OF CONTENT

1. INSTEAD OF A PREFACE

I often recall two distinct episodes of the war:

The first one took place in the beginning of the war. While breaking through the German encirclement, I lost my unit and found myself alone in a beet field. The Germans started firing their mortars in my direction. Like a rabbit, I had to jump from side to side, barely evading each shot. To mix things up a bit, Germans switched to shrapnel shells. I had to run very fast, and finally managed to escape the battery only to be taken prisoner by another German platoon.

The second episode occurred at the very end of the war. As a prisoner, I was working in the German village of Hochdorf, about two miles from the city of Freiburg. The day of our liberation, my boss 'joyfully' told me that American troops were closing in on the village and that "Hitler made *kaput*". A fellow prisoner and I went to the town hall to meet our liberators. The first car we saw had six soldiers. They were French.

Upon encountering Russian prisoners of war, they became very nice to us and made every effort to communicate without knowing our language. One soldier spoke Polish. He noticed *OST* [1] patches on our jackets (mandatory for all eastern forced laborers)

---

[1] *OST* (from the German word for East) - during WWII denoted prisoners from Eastern Europe.

1

and asked where we were from. Learning that I was from Ukraine he become very agitated, took his rifle and dragged me to the wall. A commanding corporal barely managed to calm him down, and I was saved from the honor of being executed as a Ukrainian. Had this Pole known that I was a Ukrainian *Jew*, no French general could have saved me.

These two episodes served as two mirrors each facing the other. In between 1307 days of hopelessness bounced from one mirror to the other, a horrible endless repetition of captivity and relentless nightmares.

In retrospect, I cannot understand how I managed to survive; it seems that some guiding hand gently led me through a minefield and kept me from being killed. For years I have been keeping all these memories without a chance to unburden my soul, until I received an invitation from famous director Steven Spielberg to share my memories of the Holocaust for his Shoah library.

A group of film technicians and journalists came to my house and I patiently answered their questions about my tribulations until I was fully exhausted. Later I received a tape of my interview with a thank you letter from Mr. Spielberg.

Watching this interview, I realized that I should not hold my breath for a casting call to a Spielberg movie. My interview was so bad and incomprehensible that I could not finish watching the tape. But my wife and daughter persuaded me to take pen in hand and start writing, the slightly more romantic version of what I actually did behind a computer. My dream is to see my granddaughters reading these lines.

The respected English actor and director Peter Brook once said that if his book *Memories* had any inaccuracies, it was not because he wanted to distort the truth, but because his memory was not a refrigerator and did not store his memories frozen. I think it is an author's job to weave the threads which formed the basis of his experience, so the reader can find them useful and interesting.

I have described the facts of this story not in chronological order, but in the order I have remembered them. I could not accurately tell you which events occurred before, and which later, for the darkness bounced from one mirror to the other one too many times during those 1307 days, but essential truth and facts are never distorted.

I hope that someone may be interested to learn what it means to be a Jew who lived in Nazi captivity; how one could survive while constantly expecting to be uncovered, tortured, and killed for his only crime – being born a Jew.

This is particularly important today when the old evils of fascism and communism are being replaced by a new kind of evil - religious extremism and its handmaiden, terrorism.

Still, my 1307 days of fear cannot even be compared to one second of the terror inflicted on my twelve-year-old sisters, my father, my stepmother, and my grandmother, murdered in the village of Chervonoe, Zhitomir region, Ukraine in 1941. Nor can my own dark memories compare to the horrors of six million Jews brutally murdered during the Holocaust. I always felt the breath of death, but I have survived.

2. WAR

In 1941, I lived in Kiev on Vozdvizhenskaya Street near the house once occupied by Mikhail Bulgakov[2]. During the early morning of June 22nd I remember dreaming about war, bombing and artillery fire. It awakened me up and I got dressed and left the house and went out on the street.

It was a lovely morning. There was certain freshness to the air, the smell of trees and summer. Sunshine was reflecting from the golden domes of the Andreev Church. Behind the church over the Dnieper River I saw a high-flying plane. Anti-aircraft guns were firing at it. The plane was unusual and it occurred to me that I had never seen this model before. The AAA explosions were neatly grouped to one side, quite far from the plane. I concluded that these were military exercises – the gunmen definitely did not want to damage the plane. It was very early; the city was still asleep. I was amused at witnessing such interesting military games and went back to sleep.

When I finally awoke, it was late Sunday afternoon, sunny and warm. Energized, and I decided to go to the movies. At the Passage, better known by its nickname 'The Dog Booth', they were showing a new movie, *The Space Flight*. My mood was great after

---

[2] *Mikhail Bulgakov* - renowned Russian writer (1891-1940).

the warm weekend and after enjoying the exciting new sci-fi movie about Soviet cosmonauts landing on the moon. Upon exiting the theater I saw a large crowd. The sun was bright, but disturbing shadows covered people's faces. The crowds in Kreschatik were gathering near loudspeakers listening to a concerned voice. It was Vyacheslav Molotov, the Soviet Foreign Minister.

Two generations removed from that day, I am still ashamed to admit that I felt elated to hear Molotov's announcement that Germany had suddenly attacked the Soviet Union. My seventeen-year-old brain could not comprehend the extent of the imminent disaster facing my country. Either from lack of maturity or from the excess patriotism that was surging in me at that time, I suddenly felt relief, almost jubilation.

I understood that the war would bring death and grief, but it also was clear to me that the war against the fascists was inevitable. We were preparing for conflict at schools, at work and in colleges. We passed countless certifications and tests: GTO (Ready for Work and Defense), OSOAVIAHIM (Society of Assistance to Defense and Aviation-Chemical Construction), 'Voroshilov Sharpshooter'. Soviet youth was being brought up with the belief that the enemy would be defeated on his own territory and (in the words of a popular song): *'By a powerful blow with low blood'*. Educated by these slogans I had only one thought: "Good, thank God, we finally will be able to slay this beast of fascism."

I looked at the gloomy faces around me and was only partially successful in masking my enthusiastic mood as I tried to mimic their concerned expressions. But my mind was racing. I was already planning out my strategy that would enable me to get to the front as soon as possible: I would register at my college, where I was a sophomore, or possibly go directly to the recruitment center.

I could not wait until the next day.

3. THE DUKE OF MARLBOROUGH GOES TO WAR

Nobody paid any attention to me at the recruitment center. Security guards did not even let me in. No matter - I would wait outside. Impressed by my perseverance, a sentry asked a passing lieutenant to help. The lieutenant explained to me in a friendly tone that at my age of seventeen I could not be drafted, but I could show up at six in the evening to help deliver draft notices. Perhaps by that time the situation would clear. This type of participation in the war was not acceptable to me. I had painstakingly earned the same defense preparedness pins that my comrades only one year older had earned, and feared that the war would be over before I was old enough to join. It was unfair that those who had been indoctrinated with '*By a powerful blow, with low blood*' just one year more than I had been were allowed to fight, while I was not. Nevertheless, by six pm I was there.

For some reason the draft notice distribution rules required delivery between midnight-and early morning. It was very difficult to find an addressee in a dark city. The draftees clearly did not share my enthusiasm for the coming war and some gave me evil looks. It was particularly difficult to give a husband's draft notice to his wife. Most immediately started crying.

8

The next day I went to my college and found it in complete disarray. Rumors had started spreading that everyone was to be evacuated and assigned to special schools far in the countryside. Naturally, this was also not acceptable to me. I had to go to the front and, if possible, immediately. This conviction was reinforced after I learned that my cousin Isaac, who was a few years older than I was, volunteered for a surgery to fix two of his fingers, damaged in an old accident, in order to be eligible for the draft. Isaac ended up fighting for the entire war with his two mended fingers. He was promoted to the rank of lieutenant and died in East Prussia just one month before victory. Concerned and hopeful, I listened to reports from the front. Our troops 'valiantly fought the numerically superior enemy' and surrendered one city after another.

Eventually using my local Komsomol[3] organization as a back channel I managed to get accepted into the Destroyer Battalion. My friends joked that while most people used *blat* (Russian slang for connections and personal favors) to further their careers and improve their lives, I was using *blat* to be drafted to the army.

My family, my aunt Frida and my cousins Fanya and Sima met the news with hostility. Aunt Frida started to cry. All three blamed me:

---

[3] *Komsomol* - a Communist youth organization sponsored by the Soviet Union for fourteen to twenty-eight-year-olds with a strong political indoctrination orientation.

"It is very irresponsible of you! Why don't you think about your family? Why don't you think that after all the men went to war, we need your help?"

They had very good reasons to be upset. During the first two weeks of the war all four of aunt Frida's sons: Misha, Isaac, Josef, Jan, and two son-in-laws: David and Avram were drafted to the Army. Fanya and Sima had to take care of two one-year-olds.

I felt painful sorrow for these dear to my heart women, to whom I was infinitely grateful. They gave me a roof over my head and took care of me during the most important teenage period in my life, from fourteen to seventeen.

As much as I could, I tried to reassure them:

"Please, understand: if I did not sign up now, in a few days they would send me in a far away military school and I would unable to help you. However, remaining in Kiev, not far from you, I could help when needed. Soon we will defeat the Germans, and things will come back to normal."

They accepted my arguments and calmed down. I also got my peace of mind.

After start of the war all communications with the village Chervonoe, where my father and two little sisters lived, had ceased. I did not know what happened to them.

The Destroyer Battalion was formed in order to combat saboteurs, to catch infiltrated enemy agents, to protect against tank breakthroughs and to organize civil defense.

At the time of my enrollment we had about twenty people in our unit and the headcount never went over sixty. The unit was called a "battalion" either to confuse and frighten the Germans or, more likely, to send a glowing report to superiors. The commander was a very nice young Major. Judging by his moustaches and surname, he was Georgian. After a brief introduction, he explained our tasks and, as usual, finished with political slogans:

"Your Motherland has places a great honor on you - to protect our glorious ancient city, the capital of Ukraine!"

After this slogan he moved on, leaving a corporal in command. This was the last time we saw him.

We were placed in the dormitory, twenty people in one room. For our meals we marched down the street to the canteen of the nearby Artem factory.

The first order of the day was to dig anti-tank trenches in the Svyatoshino Forest, to the west of Kiev. There were some concrete defense structures already built there before 1939. The wall thickness of these structures was barely two inches; useful to provide shelter from the weather, but not from shelling. My new battalion friends were convinced that the flimsy buildings were constructed by 'saboteurs'. The term sabotage in the 1930s and 1940s Soviet Union was applied to anything 'wittingly or unwittingly done incorrectly'. Digging anti-tank ditches on the side of dense forests was an exercise in futility. No tank would ever get near a dense forest where maneuverability and view are extremely limited and anti-tank guns hide under every bush. Irrespective of its utility, trench digging was fun, especially after local women and students were mobilized to join us.

There was a strawberry field in front of our anti-tank trench. We were allowed to eat strawberries "so they would not fall into the enemy's hands", as one women said. Never in my life have I eaten strawberries so tasty.

At night we slept in a *kolkhoz*[4] club. There was one big room for all the men and women to sleep and to rest. Needless to say there was precious little sleep and even less rest. It turned out that war and love did not interfere with one another. Sleepy and fatigued, we dragged ourselves to work each morning, but we managed to finish the trenches on time.

Before long, as darkness descended upon the forest we started noticing flashes and light flares on the western horizon. The war was approaching.

At the Karavaevy Dachi railway station, near Kiev, we worked loading trains to be evacuated to the east. This was not quite as romantic as digging anti-tank trenches but probably more useful to the war effort. Two people would put a sack of grain on my shoulders. On shaky stairs I would carry the sack onto a covered wagon where other workers would take it from me and stack it near the other sacks pushed up against the walls. Then we changed positions. We also dug trenches, learned to march, trained to shoot 45 mm. anti-tank guns and studied infantry manuals.

---

[4] *Kolkhoz* – a Soviet collective farm.

4. DEFENDING KIEV

In mid-August our platoon was assigned to defense positions near Kurenevka forest, just west of Kiev's Kirillovsky hospital. We had to dig deep trenches, gun nests, and bunkers. The deeper we dug the trenches, the more they tended to collapse because the soil was sandy and we had no bracing material. Our main weapon at this point was the Molotov cocktail[5]. They were used like hand grenades and were supplied to us in great quantities. Due to gasoline shortages, our devices were almost pure alcohol. It did not take long for this to be noticed.

Since no one actually anticipated any German breakthroughs in short order some soldiers were using this incendiary brew for 'peaceful purposes'. Uncle Vasya from my platoon initiated this 'peace initiative'. He placed the bottles on the bottom of the trench in a special pattern known only by him. The next day he carefully separated the alcohol from the rest of the explosive brew and poured it into cups for all to enjoy. Uncle Vasya's enterprise flourished, bringing him great popularity and respect. Uncle Vasya was always cheerful and had a huge repertoire of funny anecdotes and jokes, always entertaining the troops. He

---

[5] *Molotov cocktail* - an incendiary mixture of alcohol and gasoline contained in breakable containers with crude, usually wick-like, fusing attached.

was a good-natured man, about fifty years old with rich life experiences (most of which coming from his years spent in jail). We called him the 'Professor of Slang Sciences'. One of his most profound quotes went as follows: "Do not think that if you are shit, others are necessarily the same." This was his philosophy.

I liked him, but as squad leader I had to maintain the order of the platoon and maintain my own dignity. As a seventeen-year-old, this was not always possible. I was not sure if slang was allowed in a 'military unit' like ours. Sometimes uncle Vasya, having a little too much of his own 'Molotov cocktail', would start cursing superiors. Perhaps these were superiors from his old prison days, but it was not very clear whom he had in mind and we tried to shut him up and keep him out of trouble. The most effective argument was, if he did not stop, they would take away our only weapon, the Molotov cocktail. Being a patriot, uncle Vasya could not afford to lose such a valuable weapon, undermining the strength of our unit and, by extension, the country's defenses.

Once I asked him half-jokingly:

"Listen uncle Vasya, why do you drink so much? Besides ruining your health, all the anti-tank mixture you have drunk could have been used to destroy at least one hundred Nazi tanks."

"Pushkin said that the drunkenness is the Russian leisure. Pushkin was a smart man, he understood life. You are a nice guy, but still green. You don't understand. Well, if you respect me, let's drink *Brüderschaft!*"

It was very funny and I assured him of my great love. From such a long speech uncle Vasya got tired, dropped under a tree and instantly fell asleep.

By the way, the bottles we received lacked the fuses. Without fuses, they were useless, except, of course, for uncle Vasya's peaceful purposes.

Another time, when uncle Vasya was not very drunk and we were alone, I asked him why he served time.

"Because of politics" - he replied.

"Don't kid me around, tell me, I am just curious" - I asked.

"Because of politics" – he repeated. "I called a *kolhoz* cow stupid. Some party official heard it and wrote me up."

Seeing that I am dying from laughter he added:

"The less you know, the better you sleep at night. You know the saying: if a person exists, the case can always be invented.

This saying was very popular in the Soviet Union, but I thought that honest people had nothing to fear. Uncle Vasya's words sounded as a warning.

I vividly remembered one episode in 1938. I was a freshman and lived in a dormitory in a room with forty other students. One day they brought in (he literally did not come by himself) a sixteen years-old boy. This boy stood a breed apart from the rest of us with his upright head, proud posture, muscular athletic figure and very expensive suit. Without looking at anyone, he went to his assigned place. During the two days that the boy lived among us, he did not say a single word. He disappeared just as suddenly as he appeared.

We later learned later that it was a son of an arrested high ranking official, i.e. a "son of an enemy of the people".

A steamroller of Stalin terror rolled over the country, destroying hundreds of thousands of innocent people. Everyone knew something about it, but everyone was scared and kept silent. Young people were brainwashed and considered this terror to be a natural extension of a class struggle, collateral damage where the ends justifying the means.

I felt very lonely among our destroyers. For the most part they were medically infirm and elderly, which in my classification covered anyone over forty. There were some young people who signed up to avoid being sent to the front lines. As the Germans approached, my platoon started acquiring former convicts, like uncle Vasya. I was very glad when one day a new volunteer closer to my age was assigned to my platoon. His name was Misha Schwartzman.

Misha was a privileged boy. He had grown up in a well-to-do college-educated family. His parents had not been arrested during Stalin's purges. He had received a good education, loved classical music, understood the arts and appreciated literature. Our battalion was located in the Architectural Institute where many paintings and drawings were still hanging on the walls after the rest of the inventory had been evacuated. This turned out to be fortunate for me because Misha used them to teach me to appreciate art. The books were the main topic of our endless conversations. I listened to him with great interest and my only fear was that early warning sirens would interrupt our talks. Misha taught me to understand music. I still am reminded of him when I hear the Farlaf's part in Glinka's opera *Ruslan and Lyudmila*, an aria that Misha particularly loved to hum.

From squad leader I was elevated to a platoon commander. Of all the soldiers I was designated the 'most prepared for military service'. For three years in college I had taken military preparation courses and even had the experience of firing small caliber rifles. I was very proud of this appointment, but I did not know how to command. I mixed up orders and was shy in front of soldiers older than I was.

I spent the last of my money at a flea market on a used soldier's uniform and chrome leather boots. The fact that the soles of the boots were made from cardboard and would surely fall off after the first rain did not stop me one bit – it was dry and sunny outside. Instead, I gained a proper military look, so genuine that I was stopped by the first military patrol to verify my military status. This episode finally convinced me that I was a real soldier with real 'military bone'.

5. BECOMING A GENERAL

Soon I was facing the real test of my military abilities. It seemed as though my superiors had also recognized my 'military bone'. They called me in and announced that I deserved a great deal of extra responsibilities and special trust. During this difficult time, in addition to our existing Destroyer Battalion, they were creating an even tougher Special Destroyer Battalion, a special Women's Detachment that was to fight against enemy tanks should they break into the city. I was told that I would be in charge of it. My daily ration still came from the old battalion, but I had to teach the new detachment tank fighting techniques, provide political education, and teach army manuals, etc. I expressed concerns that I was too young for such a task, but my pleas were immediately rebutted by being given examples of seventeen-year–old Civil War era brigade commanders.

I was young and naïve and took everything at face value. I did not realize that most of the things around me were done just for show. I said, "Yes, Sir" (more precisely, "Yes, Comrade Commander") and went to my new assignment in a large gray building on Melnik street, opposite from what would become known as The Khrushchev Dacha[6]. The idea of commanding thirty-plus women bothered me a lot, but orders were orders.

I encountered my first problem in front of the dormitory where my anti-tank brigade lived. I could not decide whether to knock on the door (definitely not common practice in the military. Still, it was the polite thing to do because behind the door lived a different species, mysterious and forbidding to my adolescent sensibilities) or to simply barge in without knocking, thus establishing my superiority and underscoring the strength of my character. While I was torturing myself with this dilemma, fate took pity on me - the door opened and a sleepy girl went to the toilet. With upmost strictness in my voice I told her that I had been appointed Commander of the Special Women's Destroyer Squadron, and I wanted to see the whole team lined up within fifteen minutes in the courtyard of the house. Obviously, my crummy uniform and chrome boots superseded the forced tone of my voice and the girl quickly ran back to the room. Screams, laughter, and noise behind the door quickly followed.

The roll call took place, not in fifteen minutes but rather in one hour and fifteen minutes. With a most serious look on my face I paced back and forth in the yard waiting until the whole team showed up. Stuttering and blushing, I managed to finish the roll call and counted thirty-one 'fighters'. There were several young and very cute girls adding yet another reason for my embarrassment. I

---

[6] *Nikita Kruschev* - rose from his 1941 position of Commissar (a political officer in the Communist Party) to leader of the Soviet Union from 1956 to 1964.

tried not to look at them to ban any improper military thoughts from my head. I finished the lineup, appointed a corporal and attempted to start normal training.

Because of my awkwardness, it did not go well. I was confusing and mumbling my orders. The fact that the girls were not certain as to their left or right hands did not help. Whispers and hushed laughter never stopped, well calculated to further embarrass me and test my blushing abilities to the limit.

The political education did not go any better. How could I explain why our valiant troops who were dealing the Fascists such crushing blows and destroying such vast amounts of Nazi manpower and equipment, were simultaneously so triumphantly retreating?

I asked if anyone had any questions. One girl stood up and asked if they would be allowed to shoot with real bullets. I replied that the main weapon of the detachment would be Molotov cocktails, but meanwhile they could use their good looks to distract the enemy. The girls liked the joke and I was very proud of myself.

By two o'clock in the afternoon after executing a great variety of marching exercises, such as, to the left, to the right, straight, halt, company dismissed, I had exhausted my knowledge of military training and did not know what to do or say next. A corporal saved me by announcing that the entire team must report to the canteen by three o'clock; the latecomers will not get their meals. I thanked her for the reminder.

Then I issued an order, as stupid as most military orders:

"After the meal the corporal will conduct additional training exercises. The goal of the training is to ensure that all the fighters know where the left and the right hands are. The exercises will continue until everyone masters this skill!"

"Why is it so important to know where is the left and where is the right?" - asked one girl.

"Imagine that you are sitting in an ambush, and the commander issues an order to engage the enemy tanks on your right, but you do not know where the right is and shoot at your own troops. This would be a nightmare!"

The girls looked at me as they would look at the complete idiot until I told them that I was kidding. I knew there will be no afternoon drills, the girls knew it and they knew that I knew it.

My constant awkwardness and embarrassment started causing me headaches. So, when after a few days my superiors decided to release me from my Special Destroyer Battalion duties, despite the risk of causing irreparable damage to the defense capabilities of my motherland, I felt a great relief. On the other hand, it was very sad to realize that I was not fit to be a General.

Kiev was under constant bombings. Anti-aircraft guns covered the sky with flak, but the only German aircraft was shot down by our I-16 fighter. The wounded pilot landed at Red Square, in the area of Podol. Anti-aircraft shrapnel fell like jagged hale and wounded several civilians.

Newspapers and posters were calling for vigilance. After the countless show trials of 1936-1939, in which most major party chiefs and military commanders were declared spies and saboteurs, people were looking for and discovering spies everywhere. Everyone participated in this witch-hunt; it's most productive harvest being those unlucky victims were those who for nearly twenty-five years under Soviet rule did not get rid of such capitalistic finery as wearing a tie and a hat.

August brought supply disruptions. Butter, sausages and other products quickly disappeared from the stores. Our battalion had a very well stocked shop so I was able to provide some food for my cousins Fanya and Sima. When I would pass food to them through the gate that separated our barracks and the outside territory, I felt like a proud breadwinner.

As the Germans approached, the Government started mass evacuations of people and equipment to the east. My aunt Frida and cousins Fanya and Sima had evacuated from Kiev. My father and two younger sisters remained in Chervonoe, a village near Berdichev in central Ukraine. We had no form of communication and I learned of their deaths only five years later, after returning to Kiev from imprisonment and military service.

For several days it was known that Kiev was surrounded by the Germans, but no one believed that the city would surrender without a fight. There was a rally in Opera Theatre in which Marshall Budenny proclaimed that the Germans would enter Kiev "Only over my dead body." His face and demeanor projected great courage and unwavering faith in victory. Watching him I felt overwhelmed with courage and patriotism. Should he have ordered me at that moment to go under the enemy tank, I would not have hesitated for a minute. Distant artillery fire was heard from the Svyatoshino Forest area. The front was fast approaching. Our battalion began preparing for street fighting. We were taught to throw Molotov cocktails on top of the tanks, to throw grenades under the tanks and to install anti-tank mines.

Every time we went on patrol we saw how life was gradually being squeezed out of the city. The public transportation had stopped working. Streets were half-empty. The weather was miraculously sunny, but there were none of the familiar sounds of children playing in parks. All my relatives and friends had long since departed the city.

I found out that one of my distant relatives who lived on Kuznechnaya Street did not evacuate. This woman was semi-paralyzed and had to move using a self-made wheelchair. Her oldest son had emigrated to America long time ago and shortly before the war he was allowed to come and visit his mother. This was a very rare case when an American was allowed to visit and, most surprisingly, to return back to America. We were amazed that being unemployed, her son could afford such an expensive trip. Her youngest son lived with her and left her some money before being drafted to the Army. She lived in constant fear of being robbed. Her fears ended with the arrival of the Germans – they dropped a paralyzed woman from the third floor balcony.

The college was empty. The workshops where we practiced metalwork had been stripped out of all their equipment and shipped to the East.

Even before the rains started, my fears about my beautiful chrome boots came true – the soles were ready to fall off and I had to tie them with a rope. I found a shoemaker, an old Jew working from a dark basement, like in good old days. He inspected my boots, frowned, shook his head and said:

"If you want to keep your boots, I can advise you to wear them only on your hands, preferably wrapped in cloth. I will try to glue the soles a little bit, but this will help you like an aspirin to a corpse."

He glued something, knocked on something and said:

"Here we go. Hopefully they will last until you find your pre-war boots."

We started a conversation.

"I am confident that we will defeat the Germans," I said. Still, why would not you evacuate? Can you imagine what will happen to you when the street fighting starts?"

"I am an old man," the shoemaker responded. "I have nowhere to go. My grandson was in the border guard. Since the war began I do not know what happened to him. My son worked at the Lenkuznya factory. He had a deferment from being drafted. He decided that if his son is fighting, it would be a shame to hide behind his deferment, so he volunteered. My daughter-in-law is a doctor. She was drafted to the army right before my son. I have nowhere else to go. Whatever happens to everyone, will happen to me. You too did not go, so we will fight together."

After a small pause he added:

"They wrote a lot about the German atrocities, but I think that half of it is a pure propaganda. I saw the Germans in 1918. They occupied our village for a few weeks and a Lieutenant rented a room in our house. They were very decent people. He spoke to me in German, I spoke to him in Yiddish and we understood each other well. He hated the Russian way of life and praised the German culture. He said that all Russians are antisemites because Jews were not allowed to live in big cities. He said that in Russia a Jew cannot be an officer, but his own commander is a Jew, and nobody in Germany considers it unusual."

"But you are forgetting that those were the Germans, but these are the Nazis!"

"Maybe you are right, but I have nowhere to go. Here is my home."

I did not like this conversation. I thanked the shoemaker for his work and went searching for my old shoes.

The City was covered with anti-tank rails - steel girders set end-on into the ground to repel tank movement. Streets were empty. Shops greeted people with sealed empty windows. Once splendid, the beloved Kreschatik, Kiev's grand boulevard, became dull, anticipating what was to become its near complete destruction.

In a few days after the Germans entered Kiev, the whole street was demolished.

6. UNDER SIEGE

On September 18th, 1941 our battalion took position to defend the eastern edge of what in a few weeks would become the notorious Babi Yar[7]. At that time it was a deep ravine with steep slopes, overgrown bushes and narrow passages, called goat trails. Nobody expected any significant enemy force to pass through this ravine, but judging by previously built trenches on its edge, the commanders considered this area to be very important.

Perhaps from these very trenches the Germans would machine gun our people at the edge of Babi Yar in just a few weeks. But at that time it was the quietest place in Kiev.

Each of us was given an old rifle, ten bullets and a gas mask. We did not know how to fire these weapons. I received an unfamiliar foreign-made rifle with German cartridges. Apparently, our commanders were confident that these weapons were sufficient to stop the German army. There were no officers or trained military personnel assigned to our unit.

A corporal has placed us in the trenches in groups of two along the entire length of the trench and ordered not to allow anyone to enter the city without his permission. Any suspicious

---

[7] *Ba-bi Yar* - a ravine outside of Kiev where Kiev's Jews were lined up and slaughtered by German troops in 1941.

person must be arrested and escorted to the battalion headquarters, where he personally will be on duty. Anyone trying to sneak in must be shot.

With the onset of darkness we started hearing explosions and could see large fires in the area of the Bolshevik and Aviazavod factories near the railway station. The next day the distant shooting had stopped, but by the middle of the night the explosions had been heard from the eastern shore of the Dnepr River, which was considered to be deep inside our holdings. With menacing whistle the projectiles flew over our heads and exploded somewhere ahead of us. It was very strange, because by any calculations that we could make, they were our own guns firing on our own territory.

The next night was quiet and moonless. The sky was radiant with billions of stars shining down on us. Sometimes the door to some distant house would open in the valley below us, releasing a quick beam of light. It was cold and scary.

The path to Puscha Voditsa, a forest area to the north of Kiev, was usually quiet, and it seemed very suspicious when the next morning we saw a military truck driving at full speed toward us. Three Soviet soldiers from the vehicle were screaming hysterically that a terrible artillery assault had completely destroyed their unit and they were the only three who had escaped. All of this seemed very strange and because of the country's emphasis on spies and saboteurs, these soldiers were sent to battalion headquarters.

After dawn we withdrew from our positions and relocated to the police school near the Regional Hospital. The school building was wide open. We found random pieces of uniform covering the floor: khaki blouses, trench coats, *galife* breeches, police caps. We were given fifteen minutes to find something suitable for us to wear. At the end of fifteen minutes I looked like a cross between a college student (students in Soviet technical colleges wore uniforms) a policemen and a GI. I found *kirza* leather boots, blue police *galife* breeches, a gray *gimnasterka*[8] shirt and a striped *bushlat*[9].

After roll call we realized that two soldiers in our platoon had deserted. These were two young brothers who lived nearby in Kurenevka. The lieutenant, who had just been assigned to command our squad, decided in a hurry to ignore the desertion.

When we passed the dining room where we had breakfast the day before, we reminded the lieutenant that we had nothing to eat since.

Accelerate your march! You will eat your breakfast during lunch, if we ever get to our destination!"

---

[8] *Gimnasterka* - a military field tunic.
[9] *Bushlat* - a short and heavy Navy-style military trench coat.

7. FAREWELL TO KIEV

It was the morning of September 19, 1941. That day I remember to the last detail.

Shortly after dawn our convoy received orders to move toward Podol. The sky was clear and bright in anticipation of a beautiful morning. The streets were empty and quiet, but on our way past the Artem factory we saw many people running toward Glubochitsa. The entire width of the street was packed with people carrying buckets filled with some kind of liquid from sewage wells. Somebody explained that the Government had ordered the destruction of all the alcohol stocks in the nearby liquor distillery by pouring them into the sewage. This mix of alcohol even with sewage was a sufficient libation for at least some Soviet people who eagerly scooped it up and carried it away. By this fact alone we knew that Kiev was being surrendered to Germans. We did not know where we were going.

The day progressed. All the shops on Lower Val were empty after looting. Only one market on the corner of Lower Val and Konstantinovskaya was not empty and the crowd was carrying some produce from it.

Galina Leontievna, a librarian in my college, ran to me from the crowd. We had spent many hours studying in the library together and she was a good friend. She told me that during the previous night the streets leading to the Dnepr River were full of retreating Soviet troops. She was crying, in fear of the forthcoming invasion. I did not cry, but at heart I felt so bad that I found no words to express my feeling. As I was leaving, she forced two cans of crabs into my hands, apparently from the market. Crabs were considered prized delicacy. When I ate these crabs a few days later, I found them to be the most inedible food I had ever tried. I still was very grateful to Galina Leontievna for her attention.

Kiev was being surrendered to the Germans. My mind could not comprehend this. We were expecting heavy street fighting. I was imagining myself at the barricades in ambush with a grenade, ready to throw myself under German tanks. What happened was shameful and stupid, but we could not talk about it. Under the Soviet regime at that time, to doubt the wisdom of the orders was suicidal.

Without any rest our platoon reached the Dnepr River. There was a pontoon bridge across the river. It was the only bridge still standing – the others were blown up. The trusses of the nearby Railway Bridge were hanging from the towers. Nowhere in sight were Soviet military units, except for a few engineers near the pontoon bridge. We had been warned that we would have only five minutes to cross the bridge. We ran as fast as we could and in fact the bridge was blown up immediately after we reached the opposite bank. I took one last look at the right bank to say goodbye to Kiev, its green hills and white and blue Andreev Church right next to the house where I had lived.

It was so sad and painful that tears filled my eyes. This was the second time in my adult life that I experienced such a grave loss. The first time was in 1938 when my uncle Meir died. He was everything to me: an uncle, a father, a teacher and a friend. I was in Kharkov and was not able to come to his funeral because I had no money for a train ticket.

I hid my face, so that no one could see me. Misha understood my feelings and embraced my shoulders to console me.

I worried about my family left in Chervonoe - my father, my two sisters, stepmother and grandmother. My Grandma used to live in Warsaw and had already fled from the Germans to live with us.

We reached the left bank of the Dnieper around nine in the morning; I learned later that the Germans entered the city at one o'clock that afternoon.

The sun burned our skin when we reached the first rest stop in some village whose name, if I ever knew it, I have long forgotten. All the free space between houses was taken up by the troops, horses, wagons and artillery. German bombers calmly flew over us to the East, oblivious to the calamity below.

Fatigue took its toll. We wanted to drop immediately and sleep, but hunger and thirst won the battle with sleep. It was exactly 24 hours since we had had anything to eat or drink. There was no water in wells. The few droplets of dirty liquid that we managed to retrieve from our gas masks smelled of swamp and rubber.

Suddenly someone discovered a beehive in a local farm, surprisingly untouched. In a second, swarms of soldiers completely overwhelmed swarms of bees. Capturing a piece of honey wax, Misha and I sat nearby in anticipation of the feast. I managed only one bite before I felt severe pain at the base of my tongue. I spat out, but it was too late - a bee had successfully ambushed me. My tongue started to swell and soon filled my entire mouth. I almost wept from pain and disappointment.

The respite did not last long and our convoy started moving again. By night we reached the edge of a small forest. The entire forest, as far as the eye could see, was filled with vehicles and military hardware. For the first time in two days we were offered food and a lot of it. We consumed unlimited quantities of unprecedented delicacies: expensive biscuits, sausages, butter, preserves, wine, tobacco and other products, the existence of which for many of us was purely fantastical. In another time we could not even dream of such food, intended exclusively for high-ranked commanders. At this time the foodstuffs were meant to be consumed so as to not fall into the enemy's hand. This time, we got lucky.

We did not have enough bags to carry the food and stuffed our pockets, mugs and any possible nooks and crannies of our uniforms. The smart soldiers threw away their gas masks and filled the empty bags with food. Because of my swollen throat I could not eat anything, and never thought twice about throwing away my gas mask and filling the bag with food.

Our battalion was disbanded, and the soldiers were split across different units of the new division. Misha and I asked to be assigned to the same platoon. The troops treated us very well and joked about our bazaar uniforms. The overall mood of the soldiers was gloomy, but not panic-stricken. This reassured us.

After nightfall we climbed onto trucks and began moving eastward again. The trucks did not use headlights. Smoking was forbidden. The burning remains of houses on both sides of the road illuminated the way. Stalin had ordered the destruction of everything that could help the enemy.

By the next morning we had run out of gas. We dismounted and continued on foot. We saw a tremendous amount of military equipment spread for many miles: searchlights, quad machine guns, double AAA, long-range heavy mortars, armored carriers and other such instruments of warfare.

At about ten o'clock in the morning a small one-engined German reconnaissance plane flew barely above our heads. We could see the German Iron Cross on the wings and the sinister swastika on the tail. We could clearly see a pilot moving from side to side to take better pictures of us. Tens of thousands of soldiers and officers looked at this little enemy plane but no one gave the orders to shoot.

I often recall this day and still cannot understand what had been happening with the soldiers. It was similar to the way a rabbit looks at a python, paralyzed by fear, unable to move. A likely and most probable explanation is that during purges of 1937-1939

Stalin had destroyed the best part of the army command, and those who remained lacked initiative and independent thinking.

The order came to move away from the road and into a nearby field in anticipation of the coming bombers. No bombers arrived. Doubtless, the Germans did not consider us to be a viable army anymore and did not want to waste ammunition.

Finally, we moved out and deployed to the next village. Exhausted, I dropped under a shady tree and tried to get some rest. Misha helped me get to the shed where our platoon had been allocated a place for an overnight stay. Ever resourceful, Misha found some hay and arranged relatively comfortable resting space.

We rose at dawn. Misha told me that the sergeant had tried to wake me up for sentry duties, but after several unsuccessful fifteen minute attempts he had given up. Feeling guilty, I avoided eye contact with the sergeant for the rest of the day.

We continued marching for a few days until our progress halted. The Germans were everywhere; ahead, behind, on the flanks. After our forward units encountered Germans near the river crossing and suffered heavy losses, we were sent across the swamp to reunite with the main forces. The road through the swamp was very long. We were ordered to strictly follow each other's footsteps and to carry our weapons and valuables over our heads. A local guide who knew the safe passage through the swamp was leading the column. German planes flew nearby and we feared being discovered. Standing neck-high in the swamp we were an ideal target for the aircraft machine guns. By mid-afternoon we came out from the swamp to a high railway embankment which was under fire by enemy artillery. Projectiles were pounding the swamps, spraying us with fountains of dirt.

We survived the shelling and crossed the railway embankment. Within 500 yards from the embankment we saw a Soviet T-34 tank with several generals and high-ranking officers standing nearby. Someone recognized the Front Commander, General Mikhail Kirponos. The generals were watching troops on their way from one area to another.

We rested in the nearby forest. It was full of troops and equipment. Through the night the Germans had methodically sprayed the woods with mortar fire. We asked the commander of our 120 mm mortar battery why we had not responded. His reply was: "So we would not be discovered."

Everything looked like a game of hide-and-seek. The Germans surrounded us, we ran, hid, they uncovered us again, we ran away, hid, and so on.

By morning, rumors were circulating that General Kirponos had shot himself. We later learned that the general was indeed dead, but he did not shoot himself - he was killed in battle.

Some unfamiliar commanders tried to reorganize the troops. We were given the task to spread around in a chain formation, to attack the Germans and to drive them from the village located about two miles in from the forest. The commander ordered Misha and me to be in front of the attacking chain, arguing "We fight this war for you." This statement made us very uncomfortable, but it was not as if we had a choice. We moved carefully in front with the rest of the platoon following us about twenty yards behind. The words "We fight this war for you" stuck in my head.

I do not know whether it was by signal or a spontaneous eruption, but someone yelled "Hooray! For Motherland! For Stalin!", and we all rushed forward. I was thinking that the Germans would shoot in the direction of the yelling, so I ran silently, trying not to lose sight of Misha. There were few rifle shots coming from the village, but on the right flank near the newly planted forest, we were met with a heavy barrage of machine gun and small arms fire.

Our platoon turned to the forest. Someone fell. Someone shouted. Bullets whistled past my ear snapping off tree branches. Bending down as far as I could, I ran ahead in the direction of the "Hooray!" screams, because in the thick pine forest it was hard to see anything else. A fellow in front of me fell. He was shot in the stomach and asked me to finish him off. I promised to send the nurse, although we both knew that there were no nurses around.

The firing ended as abruptly as it had begun. The Germans fled, leaving only a bunch of spent shell casings. For me this victory was marred by the fact that I could not find Misha. A young lieutenant rounded up everyone for a roll call on the forest road. We had about fifty people left. No one knew how many soldiers were alive before the battle. I reported the wounded soldier but was told that we don't have time for anything except moving ahead and joining the main forces before night fell.

We started moving again. After a while we found a cart full of wounded soldiers. They explained that they were wounded the day before during the fight for the village. The Germans found them, administered first aid, put them on a cart and sent them to a field hospital. This story did not fit well with our perception of the Germans, so we looked at these soldiers as *agent provocateurs*. I could not find Misha. Afraid of becoming lost myself, I found a lieutenant and constantly shadowed him.

We took defensive positions at the edge of the village. The Germans dug their trenches near some farm buildings a little over a half mile from us and quietly waited there. Our Lieutenant evicted the residents of the corner hut and made it our headquarters. We dug trenches in a perimeter about twenty yards from the hut and made firing positions for machine guns and automatic rifles. The Lieutenant acted very professionally, setting priorities, and organizing a night watch. Around him soldiers felt confident and somehow protected from the chaos that prevailed around. He calmly explained our goals and jokingly dismissed our fears. His large frame and calm demeanor acted as a sedative to our platoon. This was the first time during our retreat that I saw a commander acting decisively and professionally.

During these days I was often sad, partly because there were no familiar faces around but mostly because I could not find Misha. As time passed by, my life became more and more organized in a proper military routine. After we ate potatoes and rested, we felt confident that we could succeed in joining our main forces.

The next morning the Germans began shelling the village. It was very scary initially. I learned to quickly bend over or jump to the ground after every explosion. By noon a German tank broke through to the middle of the village and began firing at our positions, apparently to silence our machine gun. For a moment I went to the house to get some water. In the middle of the house there was a table; a soldier was sitting there and writing. Suddenly, I heard thunder and the hut shook violently from the strong impact. After the initial shock I saw an overturned table and the soldier lying on the floor trying to get up. One of his legs was abnormally turned backwards. It was completely torn to pieces and was held together by a small patch of skin. The blood was pulsing from the wound. A tank shell flew through a wall near the window, ricocheted from the corner of the furnace, did not explode and tore the soldier's leg. The unexploded shell was lying on the floor nearby. I put a bandage on his leg to stop the bleeding, but in a few hours the soldier would die. This was the first death that I observed so closely.

After firing for a while, the tank left. The Germans continued shelling our positions but did not attack and by the next morning disappeared altogether. It was gratifying to think that they were afraid of us and retreated.

In the morning we again moved further to the east. There were no supplies. I still had some food left in my gas mask bag and I consumed it with great caution, not knowing when the next meal would come.

I ran out of bullets and reported this fact to the Lieutenant.

"Well, where do you think I can find you German ammunition? We are short even on the domestic bullets. Use your bayonet to kill the Germans and take their ammunition. He looked at my rifle—it did not have a bayonet—and sympathetically waved his hand and moved on.

It was hot. The bright sun heated my bushlat and I was exhausted. It was very hard to walk. I tried keep up, but ended up behind the main column. We passed two villages but did not see the Germans.

We stopped in the afternoon. The Lieutenant announced that he would lead the forward reconnaissance party and ordered the rest of us to follow behind. I noticed that after each village the main column became smaller and smaller, but nobody paid any attention. The demoralization process gained speed.

By the end of the day we arrived at a large and very beautiful village, part of which was occupied by some Soviet military unit with a 45 mm anti-tank gun. The other half of the village was occupied by the Germans. Our platoon had been assigned to a defense sector in a fruit orchard, near the 45 mm gun. About 300 yards of grassland separated us from the Germans. We saw them setting up a small field artillery piece and turning it toward us. In a couple of minutes all Hell broke loose. The Germans were firing shell after shell at us in rapid succession. The horses became frantic and ran around knocking everything in their way. Our guns were silent for unknown reasons, although the

Germans' positions were clearly visible. There were many of our soldiers in the orchard, all screaming, crying, and panicking. As I hugged the ground as closely as I could, each screaming sound of incoming rounds left me guessing "Will it hit, or will it miss?" I do not recall being very frightened; just simply not wanting to be hit.

After a while, the Germans directed the fire to another sector, but did not attack our positions. Clearly, they understood our psychology and did not want to waste their soldiers, hoping that we would retreat. Indeed, with the onset of darkness we were ordered to leave our positions in the village.

8. FOREST DWELLER

From that day we started our systematic drifting from one forest to another. I lost count of the days we spent migrating between the forests. We traveled on the open ground at night and hid in the forests during the day. It was very dark and constantly drizzling. To this day, I do not understand how we managed to find our way in the darkness and avoid the Germans. I moved like a zombie, half asleep, barely staying conscious if my platoon comrades walking nearby.

One night our group of about 150-200 soldiers encountered an occupied German post in a small farm. We decided to avoid this farm and not to engage in a fight. As our column moved around the farm, we came close to some bushes surrounding the road and heard a German yell: *"Halt, wer geht dort!?"* (Halt! Who goes there?) Terrified, our entire group dropped to the ground. Our reconnaissance team went ahead and determined that there were only a few Germans there, occupied with feeding horses. We carefully walked around them. The Germans, probably as terrified as we were, allowed us to pass.

People were demoralized to the limit. There were no directions from commanding officers. During the day when we hid in the woods, Germans would shout in loudspeakers: "Russians, surrender!" and "Stalin *kaput*!", but they would not enter the woods. Food was scarce. We found a lot of mushrooms, but nobody knew if they were poisonous. Some older and savvier soldiers recognized some of the edible mushrooms that we immediately plucked up and grilled over a fire. We feasted that night Even though the mushrooms were tasteless and had a sandy aftertaste. Sometimes we ventured outside to nearby fields and dug potatoes or beets.

Many soldiers lost their weapons. I had a rifle, but no bullets. The rifle was useless, but I had signed for it and was afraid to leave it behind. Our military unit was slowly turning into a demoralized and hopeless crowd. Some soldiers gathered in groups, some wandered alone looking for a place to belong, as did I. I moved from one group to another in search of friends and in hope to hear the latest news. There were many high–ranking officers in the woods, including colonels and generals. They kept their distance and would gladly yield command duties to anyone willing. Gradually, I saw fewer and fewer familiar faces. People disappeared. The nights were very cold, but my bushlat and *kirza* boots[10] served me well. Other soldiers in summer uniforms suffered a great deal more.

One such night of wandering our unit of about 100-120 people was moving from one forest to another. Suddenly we found ourselves in a clear field facing a German battery. In the field there were four German guns and piles of ammunition boxes. We were

---

[10] *Kirza boots* - low quality leather military boots.

given orders to run as fast as we could to the nearby hill. Yelling "Hooray!" we overran the battery and continued toward the hill. The Germans fled, leaving all the guns behind.

Normal commanders, at the very least, would have ordered us to destroy or disable the guns before moving on. Instead, we, like mindless lambs, ran ahead, happy that the Germans did not shoot at us. Sure enough, after we ran to what the Germans thought was a safe distance, they returned and opened fire on us from the guns we had left undisturbed.

In the heat of the attack I did not notice that I broke away from my unit and got lost in the middle of a sugar beet field. Unfortunately, I was not the only one in the sugar beet field. The Germans found me there. They trained their guns on me and opened fire. Several shells exploded very closely and covered me with dirt, but I was not wounded. Like a rabbit, I ran from side to side and jumped to the ground every time I heard the sound of an incoming round. The Germans switched to shrapnel shells. The rounds started exploding over my head and spraying me with small deadly pellets.

At that time if someone would have clocked me, doubtless I would have broken any world record in middle distance track and field, despite wearing heavy boots and a trench coat. My heart pounded heavily, trying to escape from my chest.

Eventually I was a better rabbit than the Germans were hunters. After firing six or seven shells they only managed to break my rifle's stock. Since I had long since run out of bullets, there was no reason to carry a broken rifle which I promptly discarded. At the end of the field, I jumped over some rough terrain and disappeared from the direct view of the battery. I won the hide-and-seek game where the prize was my life.

I saw three Soviet soldiers running toward the hill that we were supposed to have reached in the morning. I joined them and started running alone. While running I was constantly thinking about how to explain the disappearance of my rifle. I did not want to face a military tribunal. Suddenly, we were fired upon from the hill. I recognized the slow chatter of a Soviet Maxim machine gun. I could recognize the difference between it and the sewing machine-fast sounds of German MG42 machine guns. It was not clear whether our troops were firing at us or at the Germans located between the hill and our position. We ran to the side to avoid being hit and found ourselves in the swamp. We rushed back and jumped into a big pit or trench, apparently prepared for beet storage. In the pit there were already five soldiers and one commissar[11]. The commissar was methodically cutting off from his uniform the commissar's insignia, stars and pins. Another soldier was attaching a cotton towel, which used to be white once, to his rifle. Unwilling to believe my eyes, I asked what were they doing. In response, they pointed outside the trench. I looked outside and saw multiple groups of three-four Germans methodically walking across the field looking for our soldiers. My heart dropped. This was the absolute worst thing that could happen. This was the end.

---

[11] *Commissar* - under the Soviet system, a Communist Party official in the army unit, charged with political indoctrination and the enforcement of party loyalty.

I quietly crawled away from the pit trying to hide in beet growths until darkness. As I cleared only ten yards from the pit, I heard a German voice: *"Aufstehen!"* (Stand up). Immediately after, I felt a strong blow to my head, and lost any doubts as to whether the command to get up was addressed to me. The blow did correlate well with the command, because for a short time I lost any ability to determine where up was and where down was. Three Germans wearing green jackets with folded sleeves and armed with carbines stood over me. Shaken, I stood up. Spitting out the words *"Verfluchter Jude!"* (Damned Jew) a young soldier prepared to hit me again, but the older soldier said something and stopped him. I did not know how the Germans recognized me as a Jew. Maybe it was because I was in non-standard uniform, overgrown, dirty and, most important, I was hiding in a field. I realized that I had just minutes left to live. I did not want to die. I was overwhelmed with a sense of hopelessness, apathy and fatigue.

My Germans passed me to another German unit. They had already cleared up the pit where I used to hide and put me with a group of ten former soldiers, now prisoners of war. The Germans went ahead and left only one soldier to guard us. I was surprised when our guard carelessly put his carbine behind his back, lit a cigarette, pulled out his wallet from his pocket and started showing us pictures of his house, his girlfriend, his motorcycle, etc. Someone asked the soldier if we were going to be shot. He replied that we would certainly not be shot. Rather we would be sent to the POW camp until the end of the war. The soldier behaved very humanely, he was polite and cheerful, but I always remembered to hide the fact that I was Jewish in order to say alive. I still did not believe that I would survive, but there a small growing hope that Soviet propaganda lied about fascist atrocities.

Unfortunately, it was a rare case when Soviet propaganda did not lie. The truth was much worse than any propaganda in newspapers. But this I had yet to see.

9. PRISONER OF WAR

Meanwhile, the German unit had returned from combing the area and brought another forty prisoners. All of us were put in a convoy and were escorted to the nearby village. Suddenly one of the Germans ran to the side of the road. We heard an explosion. The German returned with his face covered in blood. The rest of the guards surrounded him, discussing something and looking at us with anger. We learned that a Soviet soldier blew himself up, preferring death to captivity. Fragments of the grenade had injured the German.

Upon reaching the village we were told to assemble in the schoolyard, which was already full of other POWs. There was a single-story middle school building. The classrooms, corridors, and porches were packed with people sitting and lying in any available corner. I found a place under the porch and started evaluating my situation. First of all, I dug a hole in the ground and hid my passport, my military ID and my Komsomol ID. I marked the place where I buried my documents in full confidence that I would return after the Germans were defeated. The captivity, the Germans – it all did not seem real and felt like a bad dream.

Very reluctantly I parted with a picture of my sisters. I did not want to do it, but the back of the photo contained my father's inscription in Yiddish and I decided not to keep such incriminating evidence.

My twin sisters at that time were about twelve years old. Fannichka, the older one by one hour, was a blue-eyed blonde, looking like a typical German Gretchen. Nyurochka, the younger one, was a gypsy-eyed brunette. When they were very young, I liked to keep their small hands in mine and would get very upset when they got bored and would try to extricate their plump hands from my grasp. They had had a very hard life. One could barely count twelve happy days among the short twelve years they had been on this earth.

They were born right before the terrible famine years of 1933-34. The hunger hit the rural areas where we lived especially hard. After the famine they became orphans. Our mother died in 1935. Mom was the breadwinner in our family. Our father did not have any skills or a profession; all his education and upbringing were intended for religious purposes. He prayed very hard, but clearly the limit on manna from the sky was depleted after Moses led his people out of Egypt. Our family had always struggled, but with mom's death the situation become unbearable. My father could not take care of his family alone and remarried. Our stepmother was as badly adjusted to real life as our father was. To save money I was sent to Kiev to live with my uncle Meir.

My arrival was a complete surprise to my uncle. He did not want me to stay with him. Upon my arrival in Kiev, he immediately sent me back to my father in Chervonoe. My father never gave up –

he had collected the last few rubles, bought a ticket, put me on the train to Berdichev and without further explanation kicked me back to my uncle.

Eventually, it was my uncle Meir who gave up. From that moment I became a Kiev resident. Despite this initial ricochet, I never felt like a stranger in my uncle's house. I was included as part of the family and everyone treated me as a native son. Only later, as an adult, was I able to fully appreciate the kindness and generosity of my uncle.

I had a headache from the blow and from hunger. After I was hit during the capture, a big bump appeared on my forehead. After some time, the bump disappeared, but it came back again on my fiftieth birthday and adorns my forehead ever since. It is my own personal tattoo and reminder.

So far, the captivity looked relatively safe, but the danger of my situation never left my mind. I could not find a way out. An escape from a poorly protected camp was possible, but where would I go afterwards? For hundreds of miles around there were Germans. Asking a local family for help was no less dangerous than staying in captivity. I lived in a village until I was twelve years old and had no illusions about locals' friendliness to my nationality.

I received my first lesson of anti-Semitism when I was about five years old. Our family rented a room from a peasant woman who lived at the edge of the village. We called her aunt Nastya. She had a soul of gold and treated us very well. When my parents went to work, she would watch me while working on her embroidery, telling me stories and fairy tales. She was as poor as we were. Her husband was killed during the Civil War[12]. She had a fourteen-year-old son, Petro, who worked at the sugar factory during the winter. He usually came home from work at three in the afternoon and would climb up to the top of the oven, which was the warmest part of the house, and where I also liked to sit. Immediately, we started a very meaningful conversation. Petro declared:

"You are a Jew."

Actually, he used a much more offensive word – Zhid. It is an ethnic slur, a fighting word; its meaning is equivalent in its offensiveness to contemporary American words like kike, yid or nigger. At that time I did not know the meaning of this word, but by Petro's tone I understood that it was something insulting and immediately responded:

"No, it is you who are a Jew."

Without getting into detailed evidence, Petro still tried to convince me:

"No, you are a Jew."

With the same conviction, I answered:

"No, you are a Jew."

This exchange lasted for a very long time, until the intervention of aunt Nastya. She would usually end the debate by yelling at her son:

---

[12] *The Russian Civil War* (1917-1922) - was a multi-sided conflict following the collapse of the Russian Empire after the Bolshevik Revolution of 1917, mainly between Bolshevik Red Army, and loosely-allied anti-Bolshevik forces, known as the White Army, including some foreign volunteers.

Why does such a big dumbass like you bother such a small child like him?"

After this I felt like the winner of the debate - my opponent was not only a Jew but also a big dumbass.

After my uncle Meir moved to Kiev (he lived there in the house built before the Revolution by my grandfather Rafail), I was already an adult - about eight or nine years old. My relationships with the local Ukrainian children were based on the same premise – constant tensions and expectations of attack or abuse. Our house stood near the road separating grabari (local peasants, transporting sugar beets) from local Jewish population. This road was a cauldron of interethnic relations.

Grabari always took the initiative. When they saw Jewish children playing, grabari would come close to the road (but never cross it) and yell:

"Stinky Jew, dirty Jew, retarded Jew" (creative translation obviously was used here).

In response, we stood on the other side of the road and replied in a similar vein, replacing, respectively, the word Jew with the word Peasant. It didn't sound bad at all. Sometimes, in support of mutual good will, we would throw stones at each other. In doing so, we tried not hit anyone on the other side.

Sometimes the grabari would move from rhetoric to violence. Once I was playing near the road with my sisters and the thirteen-year-old son of the post office supervisor deliberately ran his bicycle over my sister. I was crying from my powerlessness. The

51

wound on Fannichka's leg healed faster than did the wound of my heart.

We lived across the street from a priest. He was well respected by both Ukrainians and Jews. He was very friendly, but the children feared his black robe. The parents did not help by constantly reminding us–"Behave, otherwise the Priest will take you away!" As he approached us on the way from church, we would cautiously greet him: "Hello, father", to which he would smile and reply: "Hello, children." With a little bit more courage we would run through the gardens and backyards to meet him again and repeat the greetings process once more. We would do it two or three times in a row, but on every occasion the priest would politely greet us, smilingly accepting our game.

When my mom was alive, she always took me to our neighbors, who were local farmers. They had always been welcoming and friendly. They lived as poorly as we had, but they were living on their homeland, and we were aliens and infidels.

Jews were mostly artisan, such as shoemakers, potters, bakers, and roofers. The grandfather of my best friend Ben was a blacksmith. We pined for the privilege to help in his workshop: bringing coal, fanning the fire in the crucible and such other chores and tasks as the old man might devise. Peasants and grabari were his permanent customers. His workshop proved that Ukrainians and Jews did business together and helped each other, all the while harboring a completely uncalled for and unnecessary animosity. From adults talking around us, we constantly heard about *pogroms, massacres of Jews by nativist Ukrainians, and about the general Ukrainian resentment towards Jews expressed by the local population.*

All these thoughts were drifting through my head and preventing me from coming to a decision. I also remembered very well the recent words of my platoon commander: "We are fighting this war for you."

Incredibly, it was hard to believe that the war was going on elsewhere. After surviving the initial terrible shock of capture, people were wandering in the schoolyard looking for friends, relatives, army buddies or any familiar face. I silently prayed in my corner not to encounter any friends, neighbors or anyone else who could recognize me and out me as a Jew.

There were two wardens, one was near the gates, and the other was watching the perimeter of the yard, marked with a low fence. We were not fed, but at first the Germans allowed local residents to approach the fence and pass us bread, milk, potatoes and other products. Women from outside brought us some food and tried to learn something about their loved ones who served in the army.

An idea suddenly dawned on me, a possible way to salvation. Something in my appearance - dark hair and prominent nose - resembled people from Caucasian region and I was given the nickname "The Georgian" in college (Georgia was a Soviet republic in Caucasian region). I decided to pretend to be Georgian. With this idea I fell asleep, thus ending the longest day in my life.

I awoke early in the morning from cold, hunger and anxiety. Immediately I went to the fence in hope to get some food. There were many POWs there and the German guard did not let them come close to the fence. When he moved away, two local women gave me some sour milk and a huge piece of bread. One said compassionately:

"Look, he is just a child."

I was small and skinny and was dressed in almost complete civilian clothes.

New batches of POWs were arriving daily. Many Germans were also visiting our camp, mainly to replace their worn out boots. They would take our boots without leaving anything in place. I saw many barefoot people walking in the yard. One of the Germans tried my boots, but they were small and did not fit. Returning my boots, he looked at me and asked:

"Du bist ein Jude?" (Are you a Jew?)

I firmly replied:

No, I am a Georgian - from the Caucasus."

I did not stay Georgian for long. Some prisoner decided to bring me good news:

"Listen, *Katso*" (as Georgians call each other), he said, "There is another Georgian looking for you", pointing in the direction of my newfound fellow compatriot.

I, of course, ran in the opposite direction and hid in the corner, thinking about my next course of action. I had to drop my dream of becoming a Georgian and decided to re-qualify as a

Ukrainian. I had good credentials: I spoke the language perfectly; I knew Ukrainian folklore and their sayings and songs as well as any Ukrainian. I liked the Ukrainian literature and poetry as well as the Russian and my grades for Ukrainian classes at schools were as high as the grades of my Ukrainian friends.

I also took care of the situation with my boots: I made a small hole just below the ankles. Now every time the Germans would want my boots I would show him the hole and said: "Boots *kaput*." Everyone was satisfied.

There were no more discussions of my Jewishness.

After a while, the schoolyard could not accommodate everyone. People sat, and lay on top of each other, anywhere they could find space. This was particularly difficult for the wounded - they did not get any medical attention.

The German guards were replaced with ones from western Ukraine. The new guards spoke a mix of Polish and Ukrainian. Immediately they started the POW registration. Everyone had to provide his name, date of birth, nationality, religion and place of birth. One could easily have avoided the registration, but someone spread a rumor that the registration lists would be used to distribute bread. During registration I responded to the questions in Ukrainian and it worked - nobody suspected anything. I did not change my last name, but instead of Rafail Velvelovich I named myself Roman Vladimirovich. Given that at home I was always called Roma, a nickname of Roman, and the Germans did not care about middle or parent names, my conscience could be clear from lying.

The new guards immediately uncovered several Jews and political commanders. Some Jews were pulled by their appearance; others were betrayed by friends and colleagues. They were immediately taken outside and shot.

I was lucky. I sat in my corner and did not go outside without a specific reason. In addition, there was nobody from my battalion who could have recognized me. After several days of captivity I was still alive.

Just before I was captured, while roaming the forests, I was actively looking for my friends, co-workers, Kievans, or anyone with whom I could make friends, share the burdens and escape loneliness. Once in the camp, everything had changed – every day I prayed not meet anyone who knew me could report me to the Germans.

Meanwhile, the camp had fully been turned over to the Ukrainian police. The Germans were nowhere to be seen except when they brought new prisoners. The schoolyard could not accommodate so many people and the camp was expanded to include adjacent barns. The perimeter was marked by a barbed wire. The new police were very diligent and an escape was no longer possible.

The Germans took anywhere from 600,000 (by Soviet data) to 800,000 (by German data) prisoners in the Kiev area.

The police started moonshining. After the Germans departed, the police were never seen sober. Hundreds by hundreds, the prisoners were taken somewhere, by rumors to another camp near the town of Priluki.

The executions started. It was not hard to find a reason to be shot: failure to register, approaching the wire fence too closely, attracting the attention of a drunken guard in a bad mood. Among the crowd of few thousand people, everyone was alone with one goal - survival. People were dying from cold, hunger and wounds. The dead were buried in nearby field.

The fall brought daily drizzles. We were very cold at nights and very hungry during the day. Sometimes a few prisoners were assigned to harvest vegetables from adjacent fields. These vegetables were dropped to the ground near the gate and crowds of hungry people fought to get even the smallest piece. The police would 'restore order' by shooting into the crowd.

The camp was expanded by incorporating adjacent *kolhoz* cowsheds and barns. These buildings were shoddy even during the Soviet times and now they were completely dilapidated - peasants had stolen everything that could be removed. There was not enough space for everyone to sit. The prisoners had established a rotation order and switched every few hours to get some rest and to dry out. One of the barns had caught fire and burned to ashes in a few minutes. Nobody counted how many people had perished.

The Ukrainian police had begun to recruit helpers from among the prisoners. Apparently, it was difficult for them to drink and serve at the same time. At one time they had selected six prisoners, took them to the office, fed them, gave them drinks and offered them an opportunity to sign up for the police. Two had agreed. The remaining four were declared to be Communists and were immediately shot.

I was well adapted to starvation. I endured the famine of 1933-34. While in college, I had no financial support, except for a small stipend, barely sufficient for some bread, tea and sugar. However, even with such a solid preparation, I felt that I could not survive any longer. My head was foggy. I tried not to be seen by police, but at the same time I had to stay close to the gate, which would increase my chances of getting into the harvesting crew or finding any other job which would get me something to eat.

On one of those days of captivity, probably the tenth, but possibly the thirtieth, a cart with two German soldiers came to the gates. One of the soldiers pointed at us and ordered us to move aside. This was a sign that we were going to be picked up for some work. They asked if we knew how to care for horses. In unison, all ten selected prisoners replied, "Yes."

At that time my knowledge of horses was limited to a few facts: it was dangerous to approach the horse from the rear, unlike cows and bulls, which were dangerous to approach from the front. Nevertheless, I also replied "Yes" without hesitation. We were ordered to move from the camp to another village, a few miles away, also occupied by Germans. We were placed in several houses.

10. AMONG THE GERMANS

Another soldier by the name of Stepan and I were assigned to work for a short stocky German, who tried to talk to us in Polish. We assumed it was Polish by the prevalence of soft bumblebee sounds, but we could not understand anything he was saying and only learned his name – it was Alojz Wilczek.

My partner Stepan was a tall, square-built, handsome man of about thirty-five years old. He did not look like he was a regular soldier - it was obvious he was probably a career officer. Many career officers, especially political commanders, passed themselves as privates when in captivity.

Wilczek led us to the hut occupied by eight Germans and properly reported to one of the higher-ups. We were directed to the corner of the hut where we sat quietly, carefully glancing at the Germans. I had never previously seen Germans in normal life so close, and everything seemed strange and disturbing to me. The Germans initially did not pay much attention to us and continued talking to each other. I realized with some surprise that I could understand parts of their conversations. I realized that they were upset because their unit had taken the city of Chernigov, but the army bulletin indicated that the SS had captured the city.

After finishing their outrage hour, they drew attention to us. The main authority in this house, as I learned later, was Feldwebel Alfred Richter. Some soldiers spoke Polish to each other. The Feldwebel also tried to speak Polish to us, but he soon noticed that I understand his German better than I did his Polish. Immediately he asked me the main question: whether I was Jewish. I realized that I had made another blunder, but it was too late. Naturally, I replied that no, I was not a Jew, and even tried to express indignation over such an insulting question.

"How do you know German then?"

I explained that I had studied German for at least six years in high school and college.

He ordered me to write in German my first and last name, which I did. He gave me a German language textbook used in Soviet schools and asked me to read an article. It was about our beloved Comrade Stalin. Next it was a German newspaper. I found it to be very difficult, but managed to read something printed in Gothic font. On my own initiative, I had recited something from Goethe or Schiller. Next, I was planning some Heine poems, but quickly stopped realizing that Heine was Jewish. By the look on their faces I realized that they bought my educational claims and no longer suspected me to be Jewish. I also made a mental note to myself - never relax, even in the sleep, and always remember about the danger lurking in every conversation. Another time a German asked me if I had any Jewish friends at school and if I knew that the German and Yiddish are very similar. I lied that I did not know about the similarity of languages and that at school we never made distinctions based on nationality.

The last three years before the war had started I had lived in college dormitories and, unlike in my village, did not feel any hostilities towards me based on my nationality. My roommate was Tolya Zhuk, a very talented guy and a good friend. He was equally good at painting pictures and writing poems. I was honored that I was the only one among twenty-odd students living in the dormitory to whom Tolya would read his poems. Another student in my dormitory, Kolya Zolotarev, was from Siberia. He told me that he had never met a Jew in Siberia, but had heard many bad things about them. He was very surprised that it was rather pleasant to communicate and live with a Jew like me. Incidentally, after the war, I learned that Zolotarev was executed by the Soviets because he had become a policeman during the occupation and actively assisted the Germans to hunt Jews.

There was one very intelligent man among the Germans, and he approached us and asked whether we had eaten this day. Surprised by the unexpected warmth and attention, I dared to joke that we had not eaten today and yesterday. They gave us a thin slice of bread and some melted cheese to split between us.

Feldwebel ordered one soldier to give us a haircut, but I noticed that he paid for it from his own pocket. After the haircut, Stepan and I undressed to our waists and helped to wash each other using water from a metal mug. The Germans noticed traces of smallpox vaccinations on our forearms and made some approving comments. It appeared as though the Germans were slowly starting to accept us as civilized human beings.

Under the dim light of a small carbide lamp I carefully studied the Germans. Their faces looked healthy and nourished. Their uniforms fit very well, as if they were individually tailored. I noticed many small useful gadgets designed to help in daily soldier life: over-the-shoulder equipment belts, flasks, cases, water canteens, oil guns, etc. I was amazed at such little details like special hooks built into a jacket to keep the belt in place. Everything looked solid and well made.

When talking to Feldwebel the soldiers stood up. Feldwebel Richter was a man of average-height, about twenty-seven years old, slim, with an elongated face. His somewhat crooked nose and darkish skin made him look a little like a Jew. To our surprise, he talked to us rather graciously.

After the usual questions, like where we were from, what were our names, professions, etc. they asked who, in our opinion, would win the war. Instead of being silent, like Stepan, or merely feigning ignorance, which, after all, was closer to the truth, I jumped ahead and said that, of course, the Russians would win. I was rather scared at my unforeseen outburst, but, unexpectedly, the Germans surprised us with loud laughter.

They showed us newspaper articles describing the incredible progress of the German army. The Germans were near the suburbs of Moscow. Kharkov was captured. Leningrad was surrounded and the capture was expected in a matter of days. There was no resistance from the Soviets. My comment about Napoleon's defeat in 1812 after him capturing and abandoning Moscow was completely fruitless; no one understood me. After everything I had been through, I myself did not believe that the Germans could be stopped easily.

Before evening lights out I was told that I had been assigned to Wilczek, our work leader, and tomorrow morning he would tell me what I should do.

I could not sleep as I lay thinking over the events of that day. Instead of normal sleep, I had nightmares about interrogators demanding me to admit that I was a dirty Jew and dragging me to the gallows afterwards. I woke up in a cold sweat and could not fall asleep afterwards. I could exercise some self-control during the day, but I was afraid to say anything incriminating in my dreams. My nights become my torture and my nightmares. This continued for a long time even after my release from captivity.

Next morning before dawn Alojz woke us up and explained our duties. We were to get up before everyone else, wash and feed the horses, harness them into a cart, clean after them and prepare hay for the next day's feed.

Alojz Wilczek was either a Polish German or a German Pole from Upper Silesia. He was a farmer. Before the Germans had occupied Silesia in 1939, he had considered himself a Pole. After the annexation he declared himself a German, since Poles were being expelled from the village. Being German meant he had to serve in the army, but considering that the Germans were winning and had already captured half of Europe, this was not such a bad proposition. He spoke Polish with his fellow Poles and broken German with the rest.

I had to take care of four horses. The job, especially without prior experience, was not easy but my desire to survive overcame any difficulty. Alojz was a senior horse driver. He used to have two huge horses before – Alojz showed me their pictures and each looked as big as a house – but the horses did not fare well in difficult off-road conditions in Russia. They were replaced with four smaller but more stalwart horses, which were taken more as trophies. More horses required more servants to take care of them - I should thank these horses for having saved me from starvation.

Under Alojz's supervision, Stepan and I fed the horses, brushed them and cleaned up after them. It took a long time to learn how to harness them properly. The first day we were not given any food. They promised to include us in some ration list the next day.

After breakfast the Germans began what they called '*Drang Nach Osten*' (March to the East). A long column of German soldiers, including field kitchens and supply carts was moving northeast, deep into our country.

The day was sunny. We received an order to prepare for a parade that would be reviewed by a battalion commander. Feldwebel Richter moved two untidy soldiers out of sight. He stopped and looked at me for a moment, but then waved his hand and moved on. Just in case, I stepped closer to the horse so my unkempt look would not spoil the view. With horses as my background, I did not look so bad. The column passed the hill where a few officers stood observing the drill. The soldiers moved as wooden puppets, focusing their eyes on their superiors. When I marched past the hill, Feldwebel Richter was suddenly called to the commander. I felt a jolt inside – it was probably about me. But Richter returned back very happy and I calmed down.

In a few weeks when I started to chat with Richter, I asked him about this event:

"When you were called to the commander, I was frightened that he wanted to see me."

He laughed: "No, he personally thanked me because my soldiers looked so good."

We moved about fifteen or twenty miles per day without any resistance. The Germans always sent units forward to prepare a place to rest. Upon arrival of the main troops each unit had already been assigned to a specific house or barn.

My first day passed under stress of hunger. I could not take my eyes from soldiers who opened their stashes, took some bread, put a thick layer of butter and spam and washed it down with something looking like a coffee.

I fed and strapped the horses into the cart, but nobody gave me any food. I realized that my value was ranked somewhat below the cattle and a maybe a little above the cart. When we arrived at our destination my status had risen slightly because Richter ordered Wilczek to feed me. The cook was not happy to waste supplies on me, and reluctantly poured a bowl of soup. I instantly finished it, looked at the pot and noticed that there was some more soup left, enough for another bowl. The cook clearly did not understand my body language and said:

"In fifteen minutes after the meal you can clean the boiler. All remains are yours."

It was a pure sham. I managed to collect no more than two spoons of soup, after which the boiler sparkled like a mirror. I told the cook to count on me in case he burned soup or porridge.

"How did you learn German? Are you a *Volksdeiche*?[13]" – he asked.

"Almost. We lived in the same building with the Germans and I learned from them" - I answered.

Kurt (as was his name) bought this story.

Once my hunger subsided, my moral conflict began. I had to live among the Germans, tend after their horses and thus help them. From early years we were taught that "it is better to die standing than to live on one's knees". Only recently I had to explain to my soldiers Stalin's order: "Kill the Nazis, never surrender, save the last bullet for yourself!"

On the other hand, I did not surrender, but was taken prisoners along with thousands of others because of the failure of Soviet military and civilian leadership. Besides, from the very

---

Volksdeiche[13] – a person of German decent living in the territories occupied by Germany. They usually enjoyed considerable privileges, many acquired German citizenship and moved to Germany.

beginning I did not even have any bullets in my rifle to save for myself.

At the end of the day we received a two-day ration: a few thin slices of bread, a piece of margarine, a cheese mass and a mug of coffee. Without solving my moral dilemma, I decided to take the ration, just in case. Once we were alone, I told Stepan about my doubts. He mocked me:

"Do not go crazy. Live while you can breathe and breathe while you can live. If the Germans will not shoot you, the Soviets will. The most important thing now is to spread this ration for two days and not to eat it all immediately."

I liked his advice and calmed down, but for the entire period of my captivity and for many years after the war I felt guilty that I survived. I felt guilty standing before the fallen comrades.

The Germans continued to move forward.

Once settled in their assigned houses, the Germans, usually disciplined and good mannered, immediately changed their attitude and started systematically taking from the local population everything they could get their hands on. They called it *organisieren* (organization). Germans, who did not know a word of Russian before, quickly learned just enough Russian to demand:

"Matka dai kurku, yaiki, malako!" (Women, give me chicken, eggs, milk!)

We admired the efficiency of the peasants' 'telegraph'. The locals always knew about the German approaching well in advance and were much better prepared for their arrival than were the Soviet troops. By the time Germans would come to their village, there was hardly any food left; everything was safely hidden. The peasants were well trained to do this, prepared by long years of Soviet Collectivization, food expropriations by Communists, and forced harvest delivery quotas by Soviet authorities.

Some peasants (mostly women) were not quick enough and lost their livestock to German field kitchens. Peasants were so accustomed to this kind of thing that they did not protest at all and just stood there passively with sad looks on their faces. Some hid their animals in the forest.

Stepan disappeared a few days later. Perhaps he had found some locals who agreed to take him in as a *priymak* (adopted son). I was disappointed that he decided to escape without me. The Germans treated his escape calmly – they were sure that he would not get too far. There were no Soviet troops for many miles.

Stepan's escape reminded me again that I had to make some sort of a decision on what to do next. I was looking at all the possible options but could not pick one. It was like in the old Russian fairy tale: "Go to the left - lose your head, go to the right – lose your life, stay put – you are *kaput*". An escape would be very easy, but I was afraid of doing it alone and could not trust any of my fellow prisoners. My contacts with others were very limited. During the entirety of each day I was worked with horses with no time left for anything else. Additionally, Wilczek always gave me disapproving looks when I tried to talk to other prisoners.

I was surprised at the lack of political education and propaganda among the Germans. There was nothing like Soviet commissars and political commanders in the German army.

One of the soldiers named Leon Steiner once called me and showed me a scar on his forearm. He told me that in this spot he once used to have a tattoo of a hammer and a sickle. He was a communist from Berlin. He was unemployed prior to Hitler taking power and was a member of the communist organization, *Die Rote Fanhe* (The Red Flag). When the Nazis came to power, he removed the tattoo. The strange frankness of this total stranger caught me by surprise. I noticed that other soldiers almost never talked to him - he probably needed some outside attention. Perhaps in me, a Soviet citizen, he saw something that reminded him of the Communist fairy tale he used to believe. I asked him whether he was not afraid if others found out that he had been a Communist. He replied that it was OK, that other soldiers knew, but despised him because of this fact. When the Nazis took power and began persecuting communists, he came forward and stated that his believes were wrong, thus earning the absolution of his sins from the authorities.

Meanwhile, the Germans were moving into our territory with the precision of a well-oiled machine and without even token resistance.

As the Germans moved eastward, their extended supply chain had deteriorated and the rations were reduced. The *Organiziren* did not work anymore. While in the Ukraine, the Germans could find prosperous villages where they were warmly greeted. In Russia, however, there were only poor villages filled with beggars.

Caring for horses took most of my time and energy, but even during rare opportunities for rest I still tried to stay near them. I felt more secure around horses. Horses did not ask questions. Around them I did not have to monitor my speech to filter out any possible Jewish words or expressions.

The soldiers did not care about me. The only person expressing any interest was my owner - Alojz Wilczek. He cared about me to the same extent that he would care about other valuable inventory such as horses, saddle, harness, or wagons.

One exception was another soldier named Polachek. He was a tall, square-built fellow with rosy cheeks and a handsome face. Like many other soldiers, he was from Upper Silesia and spoke Polish. Between his hostile glances and whispers, *"Verfluchter Jude"* (Damned Jew), in my direction, I did not have any doubts about his attitude towards me. It was very logical that his last name sounded like the Russian word *Palach* (Executioner). He volunteered to perform executions of POWs at each opportunity he received, and did so with great enthusiasm. He left me alone only after he was reprimanded by Feldwebel Richter.

The horses were my closest companions. They also were prisoners of war. They treated me well. When I approached, they would synchronously turn their heads toward me, looking at me with knowing eyes and quietly sighing. Honestly, they were probably sighing because they were hungry, so I was not quite sure that their relationships with me were totally selfless.

Among my horses one gelding stood apart. The Germans called him Fritz. Like the Russians, the Germans liked to give their animals human names. Despite such an embarrassing name, we clearly sympathized with each other. When I approached him and he was not busy eating, Fritz would touch me with his lips and tickle me. I assumed that in the horse world this constituted as kissing.

As is often the case among people, those who we love the most tend to hurt us the most. One day Wilczek told me to take Fritz to a blacksmith to fix his horseshoe. Without any prior experience and with no directions from the blacksmith, I raised the horse's hind leg. Fritz had probably decided that I wanted to hold him, so he immediately transferred to that leg all the weight of his body. I still cannot understand how I withstood twenty minutes under a load of a horse. I can only remember the Germans laughing unbending me after work. I hated Fritz for a few days after.

11. FELDWEBEL RICHTER

In a couple of days after Fritz almost killed me, I was told about changes in my duties. Two horses, including Fritz, were taken away from me. Instead, I was given a riding horse for Feldwebel Richter and was ordered to be his servant. I had to clean his boots, jacket, bring him hot water to shave, wash his dishes, etc. Instead of four horses I had to maintain three horses and one Feldwebel.

This change was not only quantitative but also qualitative. I was initially offended to be a 'lackey', but soon realized the full benefits of my position. The Germans, with their tendency for deference, almost immediately started treat me as a member of the 'Emperor's Entourage'. Polachek stopped his malicious whispering. When I cleaned Richter's boots, I felt the soldiers were ready to formally salute me. (In all honesty, I could have been mistaken - the soldiers could have been ready to salute the boots.) These new duties were not burdensome, but my position had a negative side – I could not hide among my horses and being among the Germans was fraught with danger.

I remembered one conversation with Richter, after which his attitude towards me changed. He asked me who I had been before the war. I replied that I was a student at the mechanical engineering college.

"What did you study in college?" he asked.

I told him that we studied physics, chemistry, mathematics, literature and many other subjects. He became interested and inquired further. Confusing German and Russian words, I tried to tell him about physical phenomena in nature, the stars, the structure of the Universe, the Darwin theory and a number of other things. Sometimes, encouraged by his attention, I drew graphs, charts, equations. It was very strange, but he showed genuine interest in my stories.

My favorite activity before the war had been reading. For me this was more than a hobby - it was my life. I left all my friends in Chervonoe and since then had not acquired new friends in Kiev.

Books were my only entertainment. I checked them out from the library and gulped them down in large numbers. I stole candles from my aunt (we had no electricity in our apartment) and read until three o'clock in the morning. I read in the classroom and even learned to read while walking. It was only during my literature, physics and mathematics classes that I did not read. Balzac and Thomas Mayne Reid (an American author of British origin who, oddly, is almost unknown in the American academic community, but very popular at the time in Russia), Dante and Jules Verne coexisted in my head, not to mention Pushkin, Lermontov, and Korolenko and others. I loved the Fun Learning books by Perelman. I was reading in my spare time and I scarcely had time to prepare my homework.

As I was observing the Germans, I was surprised to find them very limited in their education. I had thought that in Europe, especially in Germany, everyone must have been very well educated, but later found that the soldiers lacked knowledge of absolute basic things. They had little interest for anything outside their trade. One soldier, a young eighteen-year-old fellow named Moritz, was not able to read or write. Before the war he had been a shepherd in the mountains. He sang folk songs beautifully and yodeled perfectly, but otherwise he was uninformed and illiterate.

Feldwebel Richter was a carpenter in his civilian life. He was a little bit ashamed of his lack of general education and did not want to discuss it. He considered people with better education to be members of a higher caste. He was mostly unemployed between the wars and at the first opportunity he signed up to the *Wehrmacht*, once it was allowed by the Versailles Treaty. He was very flattered when I said that carpenters, especially fine woodworkers and finishers like him, were the elite group of the Soviet working class and this occupation was very prestigious and better paid than engineering work.

Before going to sleep, the Germans usually engaged in the sport of lice hunting. Lice were everywhere: in underwear, clothing, hair, blankets. Germans sat half-naked around a carbide lamp, picking lice. They called lice the 'Russian secret weapon'.

Germans constantly complained about the backwardness of Russian life - dirt, cockroaches, lice, the lack of basic amenities in the homes, the lack of roads. They could not comprehend how entire Russian families, adults, elderly and children, would sleep together in one room and blamed Communists for this poverty. At the same time they praised Hitler for ending unemployment in Germany, raising the living standards and restoring order in the country.

I took their complaints about Russian life and Communist ideals as personal insults. I tried to justify the backwardness on centuries of Tartar Mongol occupation, on the distance from the rest of the world's trade routes and on the legacy of the Czarist rule. I proclaimed that under socialism, life was getting easier, that education and health care were free, that there was no unemployment, and, as Stalin had said, "Life is better now, Life is more fun."

I hated the Germans as enemies and conquerors, but at the same time I was jealous of their strength and ability to live well. I also hated their false God-fearing attitude and fake integrity.

In the Soviet army, we had been accustomed to having daily politics classes, but the Germans had nothing like it. Their only contact with politics was through newspapers and magazines. Soldiers exchanged views freely and often criticized some events, sometimes in abusive terms, but they never talked disrespectfully about their superiors or about Hitler. They talked about Hitler in the same way we talked about Stalin. The tales about Hitler's mythical powers were widespread – soldiers believed that no one could withstand the strength of Hitler's handshake.

Almost none of the Germans read newspapers. The preferred illustrated magazines, that contained jokes I did not understand and drawings of naked women.

Once I noticed a small ten-page booklet in the pile of newspapers and magazines. I cannot remember the exact title of this brochure, but recall noticing a stamp that read "For Internal Use Only". I did not see anyone reading it and out of curiosity 'accidentally' took it to the stables in order to read later.

This thin booklet perfectly described all the inhumane goals and ideals of Nazism. In ten pages were laid out the goals of the German Army and directions to the German soldiers. Everything I read in this book I had already known from the Soviet newspapers, but I still could not believe that such abhorrent ideas could be printed directly on paper in such a straightforward way and so cynically and shamelessly promoted.

The booklet stated that the task of the German army was the seizure of all Eastern lands up to the Ural Mountains[14]. Polish and Russian populations must be eliminated, except for a limited number of people necessary to service German colonists. The Ukrainian people must be Germanized and in time merged with the Germans. Ukrainians who would not acquiesce would be destroyed. There were many chapters dedicated to the steadiness and determination of German soldiers, the courage and the loyalty, and the great mission of the German people. I remember one particular part - German soldiers were forbidden to engage in sexual relations

---

[14] *Ural Mountains* – a mountainous region separating Europe from Asia.

with Russian women, since the children of such relationships would improve the Russian race.

This booklet said nothing about Jews. Instead, this topic was covered daily in every newspaper. Everyone who Nazis did not like was declared a Jew: Lenin, Roosevelt, Stalin, Churchill and many others.

Especially repugnant in its virulent antisemitism was *Der Sturmer* (The Storm Trooper) newspaper. The front page always began with the slogan, "Jews Are Our Enemies" and ended with another slogan, "Jews Started This War". The next page started with: "All Jews Are Thieves". And so on until the last page. The newspaper was filled with hysterical crazy nonsense intended for complete idiots.

The newspaper described and published pictures of happy Jewish life on designated reservations. It described the ways to uncover a Jew by examining their specific eye patterns. It discussed how to deal with Germans not willing to abandon their Jewish wives – the answer was unambiguous - treat the spouse as you would any other Jew.

At this point, I had not read anything crazier in my life, except after the war during Stalin's crusade against 'Cosmopolitan Jews' and during the 'Jewish doctors' affair'[15]. All this later

---

[15] In 1948-1949 a number of prominent Soviet Jewish intellectuals were accused of collaborating with international Jewish organizations. This marked a start of virulent officially-sanctioning antisemitic campaign which reached it heights in 1952 when a number of prominent Jewish doctors were falsely accused of poisoning high ranked Government officials, leading to preparations for mass deportation of Jewish population to Siberia. Stalin's death interrupted these

virulent hatred of Jews and other peoples was clearly based on the German chauvinism I was encountering at the moment.

Goebbels wrote about Germans and the German people in exactly the same terms Soviet propaganda used to write about Russian people in 1950s: everything good in the world was invented by the Germans. The Germans were declared to be *'Das Folk der Dichter und Denker'* (People of Poets and Thinkers). Einstein's relativity theory was condemned as 'another Jewish lie'. Music by Jewish composers was banned and books by Jewish authors were burned.

Newspapers constantly bombarded their reader with tales of the superiority of the German race. They extolled German spirit, perseverance, loyalty to the Fuhrer and brutality against enemies of the Reich. I remember one paragraph, which, I believe, is a key to understanding how the consciousness of the whole German generation was the poisoned:

> *"Halte dir stets for den Augen*
> *Das du ein Kind des tapfersten*
> *Und fleisigsten Folke der Erde bist,*
> *Das durch fiel Muhe und Opfer*
> *Zu seinem Ziele kommen must."*

(Remember constantly that you are the child of the most courageous and hard working people of the Earth, and through hard struggle and sacrifice you will achieve your goals.)

---

plans, but the official antisemitism never subsided until the collapse of the Soviet Union.

I have remembered the essence of this verse for the rest of my life. This is how the whole German youth generation was brainwashed.

Because of their illiteracy and lack of interest in newspapers, the Germans around me were less affected by this propaganda. This, I believe, could explain their rather tolerant attitudes towards me. Another contributing factor was the protection of my 'patron' Richter. He did not try to intentionally or unintentionally expose me, but I always understood that my life was hanging on a thin hair, which could be broken by one wrong step or word.

I felt that Richter suspected that I was a Jew. Sometimes he even jokingly called me 'a Jew'. He loved to tease me and to provoke a dangerous dispute, and being a complete idiot, I often bit on his challenge, oblivious to the lurking dangers. He once said that the Germans are the top race, the *Herren* (Gentlemen) and the victors, and the Russians are the lower races, the *Narren* (Fools) are the losers constantly on the run from the Germans. This was said in jest, and should not have been offensive to me, since I pretended to be a Ukrainian, and in the German ranking the Ukrainians were closer to the *herren* than to the *narren*. Rather than remaining silent, I innocently asked if it was true that both of these words sounded and were written almost the same, except for one letter. He laughed and said, *"Schlau du bist wie ein Jude"* (You are as smart as a Jew).

Thinking about those days, I try to understand why Richter tolerated and even patronized me. I think that initially I triggered the same reaction in him as a small puppy would, that of amusement and helplessness. The Germans were drunk over their victories, felt strong and could afford to be good-natured. When I remember Richter's attitude towards me, I cannot elude from the feeling that he greatly contributed to my survival; he was my Schindler. When I emigrated from the Soviet Union to the USA many years later, I tried to find Richter through the German consulate and thank him. I received a reply stating that according to Red Cross records, Richter had died after the war in the Soviet POW camp.

As time passed by, after the Battle of Stalingrad, after the German were defeated near Kursk, Richter, clearly remembering our first conversation, asked me who would win the war. This time around I replied that, of course, the Germans would win. By the look in his eyes and the tone of his question, I realized that any different answer would have had dire consequences for me.

After sundown I had to stay indoors. I was able to venture outside only under escort of a soldier. All of the prisoners were supposed to wear armbands with a red stamp *WH* (Property of the Army). The same stamps were used to mark horses, harnesses and other equipment.

12. MARCH ON MOSCOW

The Germans continued their unopposed march to the Northeast, but they had to slow down because of the rains. The roads become swamps. The Germans were dirty and hungry; their supply lines were completely disrupted. They cursed Russia, its poor roads, the war and anyone who might have played a part in the reduction of their already meager rations.

During the march, the Germans usually kept to the dry side of the road, or moved to the field jumping from one dry patch to another. I had to walk beside the horses in the middle of the road. My cotton bushlat become so wet that it had more water in it than it had cotton. It never dried overnight. My feet slipped in the mud and tended to get under the wheel cart. Sometimes I became stuck in the swamp, barely managing to drag my feet out, risking losing my boots.

Obviously, I got sick. One day I was feeding horses after a long and difficult march and I started coughing and spitting blood. However, it was dark and I was not sure, so I decided to test myself by coughing in my hand. My palm became covered with blood. I was afraid that the Germans would notice and while in their presence I tried to suppress coughing and would swallow the mucus rather than spit it out. I felt an acute pain in my chest and under my shoulder blade. My legs could not move and my head was in a constant fog. It lasted a couple of weeks.

When the frosts came, I started feeling better. My coughing up blood had stopped. The war was a quick and radical doctor. *(The symptoms came back several times, the last time in 1967 when I had to spend one month in the Kiev Tuberculosis Institute).*

Germans had reached the highway and accelerated their movement. The only sign that the war was not over at the end of November was a lone Soviet bomber. The aircraft dropped two bombs and disappeared. We met the Red Army in December near the town of Livny. The German convoy with the supply chain, the kitchen and the full staff approached the city, fired from their cannons and machineguns took a few prisoners and captured the town.

More specifically, these were not prisoners of war but deserters. They had no weapons. There was no fighting in the vicinity. I had no sympathy for them as soldiers, but felt sorry for them as human beings.

Polachek immediately shot four prisoners right in the middle of the city. He took their trench coats and hats with earflaps, which, due to the harsh winter, had become very popular with the Germans. Then Polachek ordered the prisoners to go toward the woods and killed them with his machine gun. He did it with visible pleasure. I had heard talk among the Germans about the order to shoot all prisoners, because it was complicated to transport them back. In the few days that we had stayed in the town I could see the bodies of the unfortunate soldiers lying in the middle of the street. Scared residents were afraid to approach and bury them. They were not the Jews or commissars, that the Germans so hated. They were ordinary elderly Russian peasants.

It became colder and colder. We reached the city of Elez. Everything went the same way as in Livny. Germans fired a bit and entered the city. Unlike Livny, where burning houses met the Germans, Elez was quiet and deserted. All the homes were intact, shutters and gates were closed or nailed down. The beautiful and ancient Russian city did not want to greet the invaders. A majestic cathedral stood in the center of the deserted city. Rare snowflakes were falling on clean paved streets. It was quiet and solemn, like in a house where someone had just died. At this time, the Germans occupied only one half of the city, up to the river. On the other side of the river the Russian were holding steady their positions. The river was not frozen yet and we were ordered to take the horses down to the water to drink. The Germans had set up machine guns and stayed hidden behind us. The other bank was silent.

Another horse servant Vanya and I were placed in a two-story house on the outskirts of the city. The house looked like it had been hastily abandoned. The oven was still warm. There were many books on the shelves, mainly political. We were forbidden to go out without permission, except to the shed to care for the horses.

One night, a Russian soldier had defected to the Germans. He was holding some German leaflets and was saying something about the Geneva Convention. He was passed on to Polachek.

I remember the next day down to the last detail. It was the end of the German Blitzkrieg and the beginning of the end of the German Reich. The day was overcast with a light snow. Not one soul was on the streets. Not a single shot was fired from either side. Everyone was consumed with a nagging anticipation that something significant was afoot. We were sent again to the river with the horses, despite the fact that there was plenty of water in our kitchen's faucets. Our backs felt the German machine guns aimed at us.

In the evening, at about six o'clock, we were ordered to harness the horses and to do so in absolute silence. It was forbidden to turn on the lights, to light up the matches or to smoke. The German convoy very quietly and with typical Teutonic order withdrew from the city, the same way a thief leaves the apartment he has just robbed.

I do not remember the exact date, but I now realize that it was the most significant day in the country's history.

13. THE GERMANS FLEE FROM MOSCOW

The German defeat and their subsequent departure from Moscow were chronicled under the euphemism 'frontline alignment' in the newspapers printed in Germany and by the local *Wehrmacht* organization.

Beginning quietly and peacefully, the 'frontline alignment' had morphed into loud fireworks in front of the moving German convoy. Tracer rounds pierced the dark sky, sounds of artillery fire and shell explosions pierced my ears, dark tank silhouettes were lurking ahead. By the following morning, the shooting was much farther away, but the Germans continued moving without rest. The Germans moved across raw fields, the falling snow helping to hide their moving columns. The soldiers were extremely tired with some dropping in their tracks from exhaustion.

Rumors started that the Germans were surrounded. The order came to burn anything that could be burned in order to halt the advance of the Russian troops. The Germans held defensive positions during the day and retreated during the night. The road was illuminated by burning villages. We could only guess what had happened to the residents of these villages. The burnings did not achieve their intended goals and did nothing to stop the Russian advances. The Germans become very gloomy and started cursing the war, the cold, their superiors and everything else in the world. The most popular words were *shaiss* (shit), *donnerwetter* (damn it) and *Verfluchter* (damned).

In a few days time we passed a village, where Russian partisans had destroyed the German headquarters shortly before. The dead German soldiers were lying everywhere among burned cars, houses, gas masks, weapons, documents and maps. Apparently, the Germans were killed in an ambush, since I did not see any dead Russian soldiers. This picture of total defeat was very impressive.

Soldiers talked about the division commander General Kohengauzen killing himself because he did not agreed with Hitler's plans to attack Russia. According to other rumors, the General had been killed by partisans. Either way was fine with me. It was very indicative that such talks, unthinkable just three weeks ago, quickly spread among the Germans. The pictures of destroyed German units vividly reminded me of very similar pictures of three months old defeated Soviet troops, but this time around my feelings were completely opposite.

The 'frontline alignment' lasted many days. There was no supply of new provisions. Soldiers were allowed to eat their emergency reserves. A deep snow hampered any fast movement. Many soldiers suffered from frostbite. Former communist Leon had been killed during a night battle with the advancing Russians troops.

Our situation had become much worse. Before we had used to enjoy some freedoms, but now the Germans controlled our every movement. We were not allowed to venture outside the gate without a guard. Sometimes I was locked inside a shed with horses.

Through gaps in the walls of the shed I could see what was happening outside. Russians used tracer bullets to burn down the house where the Germans lived. The flames made the night as bright as day. I could see green German trench coats on white snow. Pain filled my heart when I saw how many Russian soldiers were left dead in front of German machine guns.

The intense shelling started. During one such attack a projectile hit the shed where I was staying with the horses. One horse was killed and my former friend Fritz was wounded. A huge metal piece of shrapnel punctured his abdomen. The horse whimpered frighteningly. Fritz was sent to a veterinary hospital and returned in one month with a stitched stomach.

In the morning the attacks stopped and the Germans started their usual "frontline adjustment".

Now, in addition to the danger of being shot by the Germans, I enjoyed the added risk of being killed by my own troops.

In one of our conversions, Richter half-jokingly asked me whether I wanted to escape. Not expecting a meaningful response from me, he added:

"I do not recommend it. We may be taken as prisoners, but you certainly will be shot."

I said that I knew this and advised him to remove his *Deutsche Kreuz* (German Star) medal if he were to be captured. The *Deutsche Kreuz* was a huge badge on his stomach, very colorful and with a large Nazi Swastika in the center. He was very proud of his medal.

I understood that he was right. Once in our territory, I automatically became the 'enemy of the people'. I knew about a special service in the Soviet Army called SMERSH (short for 'Death to Spies') created specifically to deal with deserters, spies and POWs like me. At best I could expect to be assigned to a punishment battalion and to 'pay with my own blood for my guilt to the Motherland'. At worst, I would be shot. Thus, the only choice I had was whether to die in German or in Soviet captivity. Miraculously, I was able to hide my heritage for the entire three months, but I could not count on such miracles to continue once I would be on the Soviet side.

Despite the looming danger, I was very grateful for the success of the Soviet troops. Even when I was under Soviet shelling, I watched with pleasure as the Germans hid and ran for cover.

In early January the Germans managed to break out of the encirclement and stop the Russian advance somewhere in the Orel region[16]. Tired and exhausted our unit was sent to Orel for a few days for rest and replenishment. We came to the city at night, crossed the bridge and stayed on the outskirts of the city.

---

[16] The *Orel* Region is located in the southwestern part of European Russia.

We were all sent to take a bath. I do not remember under what pretext, but I managed to avoid this potentially deadly procedure – if my circumcision was discovered I would not see another day.

The Germans had a late Christmas celebration in January of 1942. Many received their presents from home: beautiful cards and cookies hardened after a long trip.

One soldier brought a local newspaper in Russian. It was a one-page leaflet with a tremendous amount of misspellings and grammatical errors. Besides a few messages about the German army victories, the page was full of the usual curses directed toward the Jews. I remember this puny newspaper only because of one particular article, a literary critique of the *One-storied America* book by Ilf and Petrov[17].

After several months in retreat our German uniforms started falling apart and the soldiers looked pitiful – unshaven, dirty and withered from cold and hunger. Our horses were supposed to be inspected. We had to clean them and make them shine. I worked for hours with scrapers and brushes, trying to please Wilczek, but my hungry and thin horses did not want to shine.

After the inspection ended we were sent to the frontline. We began marching again, passing the territory that had been occupied

---

[17] *Ilia Ilf, Evgeniy Petrov* - renown Soviet writers-humorists, who in 1935 co-wrote a singularly insightful book about their trip to the USA (Ilia Ilf was Jewish).

by the Germans since the summer. The original poverty of Russian villages was aggravated by German occupation. It was scary to look at the people, especially at the children. Covered in dirty washcloths, the children looked at the outside world with hungry and frightened eyes. I did not hear any children crying. Looking at them I thought about my sisters, but I it had never crossed my mind that they were not somewhere, in some village, looking at some scrawny POW with the same large frightened eyes; it had never crossed my mind that they had been simply, brutally, murdered.

A few days later the Germans took defensive positions near the town of Zhizdra, in the Bryansk region. The village was previously destroyed almost completely and some buildings were still burned. The snow was indistinguishable from the night sky - it was completely blackened from Russian artillery shelling.

The front line had stabilized. All of us - horses, prisoners, and guards – were sent to the POW camp. It was mid-January, 1942.

14. AMONG MY OWN

This concluded the first phase of my life as a prisoner among the Germans. Indeed, for the first three months of captivity I mainly lived among horses and the Germans; now I had to live among the horses and prisoners like me. The time in captivity seem like a continuum of hunger, fear, cold long nights followed by equally miserable days. From the total of 1307 days I spent about 120 days among the Germans, another 200 days in Germany, and the remainder in POW camps.

Frankly, I was not sure where I would face greater danger – acting as an imposter among the Germans or acting as an imposter among my own people. I barely managed to fool the Germans and hide my nationality. Knowing well how the Soviet 'Friendship of Peoples' worked, I did not have any illusions about the chances of surviving among my own.

The camps I went through varied by the number of people occupying them, the organization of security and the nature of the work they were performing. A lot depended on how long the camp was in operation. Sometimes the civilian forced laborers were brought in. In all cases, the guards were Germans: soldiers from the second–line reserves or otherwise temporarily exempted from the service (*Inner Dienst*), stablehands and field gendarmes.

The guard and stablehands lived outside the camp and came only to supervise and inspect the work. The prisoners were forbidden to go outside the without escorts. In several cases prisoners went outside (on purpose or inadvertently) and the guards opened fire without warnings. It should be noted that unlike the field gendarmes, the guards were not bloodthirsty. This was understandable: we were working livestock.

Our main work was to care for the horses and to transport cargo. In winter we had to gather firewood and use it to clear and repair the roads.

The first camp was situated somewhere in the Bryansk region, about twenty miles from the front line. I was there until late summer, 1942.

They brought us to a shattered village. The guards occupied a few surviving houses, the Field Gendarmerie having taken the biggest one. Were told to take apart broken houses and build shelters for the horses. For ourselves we built mud huts by digging holes in the ground and covering them with remaining what scraps of wood we could salvage.

The guard consisted of regular soldiers and field gendarmes. The gendarmes, dressed in long rubberized raincoats with metal chains and huge medallions on their chests, inspired an impending sense of horror in us. It looked like the German soldiers were also afraid of them. As a rule, no POW arrested by gendarmes had ever returned. One time, I was cleaning their house. By that time I had already learned that it was better to be as inconspicuous as possible and to not show any signs that I knew German. I successfully drew no attention to myself as I managed to overhear the gendarmes talking to each other.

One of them complained, "You know, unlike others, the Jews are very troublesomely when we shoot them. They always resist or try to escape."

A second gendarme concurred. "Well, what do you want? They are cultured people", he reasoned logically.

With all my energy I continued mopping the floors so they wouldn't think that I was also 'cultured'. When I finished he praised me, *"Gut, du bist ein guter Russe"* (Good! You are a good Russian).

The rations were sharply curtailed. If before I always was semi-hungry, now I went totally hungry. I learned to steal oats from the horses. The kernels were quite eatable. Sometimes when we found a dead horse, we smuggled pieces of meat, hid them from the Germans, boiled them without salt and ate everything, wondering how steppe people ate this disgusting stuff.

I had befriended a few fellow prisoners. The most intelligent among them was Leo Klein, a Soviet German from the Volga region. Like most of us, he was captured near Chernigov and was also assigned to the horses. He was a tall handsome guy, about twenty years old. He spoke fluent German and the Germans treated him respectfully. He stayed with us until March of 1942. Some German officer had invited Leo to his home in Germany. He returned from Germany as a German soldier, and clearly felt uncomfortable when meeting us in his German uniform. Perhaps he was a 'good communist' in the past and could not easily adjust to being a German soldier. In 1943 he was killed near the town of Rechitsa in Belarus.

I have to mention here Ivan Titov, with whom I had the privilege of being friends for a long period from February 1942 until mid-1944. As much as we could, we assisted each other living through the burden of captivity. Vanya was working under a German who was a friend of my master Wilczek. Because of this relationship, Wilczek did not mind my friendship with Vanya. Vanya was twenty years old, but looked much older. He did not like to talk and had never disclosed the details of his capture. He had only completed middle school, but his lack of proper education was well compensated for by his natural intelligence. He carefully crafted each word and spoke calmly and persuasively. The more time I spent with Vanya, the more I liked him and the more I was becoming attached to him. I gained a dedicated, honest and caring friend who stayed with me until June of 1944 when we both got injured and separated.

All prisoners were unified in their hatred of the Germans, but any talk about escape was unthinkable. Nobody trusted anybody. Vanya was the only person with whom I eventually discussed the possibility of escape. Of course, I never mentioned that I was Jewish. Vanya, in his usual manner, exhaled deeply, took his time to respond, waiting until the time when none of us could be heard, and advised me to throw the idea out of my head. He described one event that he had witnessed in the Soviet Army, before his capture by the Germans. A group of Soviet soldiers under a young Lieutenant broke through the German blockade and joined their comrades in the Soviet battalion. All of these soldiers, including the Lieutenant, were immediately shot as traitors in front of the troops, only because they came from the 'occupied' territory and were not to be trusted.

We were unable to control our own destiny and we were waiting for a miracle, and miracles were in precious short supply.

We lived in mud huts, eight or ten people in each. The horses were housed in nearby sheds. I cared for three horses: my old friend Fritz, Richter's personal horse and one cute but very nervous gelding with no name. Like us, horses suffered from hunger. It was physically painful to clean them - our scrapers and brushes bounced off their bony sides. All the horses were infected by lice, which created extra difficulties.

Feldwebel Konrad Shtopke was our camp commander. He was a fat and heavy German, a great lover of beer and horses. There was no beer but plenty of horses. Every week he organized horse inspections and God forbid if a horse was ill, dirty or hungry. Shtopke's eyes would become bloody red and he would start screaming in a mixture of Polish and German. However, to his credit, he only managed to scare us and never passed us to the gendarmes. This Feldwebel was tireless in his search of work for us. If he saw anyone idling, he took it as a personal insult.

As I mentioned before, I could easily fool the Germans by saying that I was a Ukrainian or a Georgian. As for our people, after going through endless circles of lying, collectivization, food confiscation, production quotas, and the Terror of 1937-1939[18], could not be easily fooled and suspected everybody and everything. I realized this from the very beginning.

Once, when our whole group was sitting in a mud hut picking lice under the dim light of a carbide lamp, one of the prisoners, Petya Komissarov, said to me:

"Listen, Roma, they say that you are a 'Blackass'."

I was not sure what he was referring to. The word 'Blackass' was usually applied to African blacks and dark-skinned inhabitants of the Caucasia region. Perhaps the Jews were also counted as blackasses.

Komissarov was dim-witted, but otherwise quite good-natured and harmless. He could hardly have thought of such a question by himself, without being prompted by this topic being discussed among his fellow prisoners. A nervous silence followed and I was lost for a while not knowing what to answer. Then I responded:

---

[18] In *1937-1939* Stalin initiated a campaign of terror, show trials and extra judiciary executions, mostly by fabricated charges. At least one million people were executed and millions more sentenced to years of hard labor in Siberia. The mass repressions initially affected ruling military and political elite and extended to successful farmers 'kulaks', 'dangerous' ethnic minorities, family members of oppositions, military officers, intellectuals and industry management.

"Why don't you lick my ass with your tongue? Then you could see if it is black or white. Should I take of my pants off now?"

"No, no rush", answered Petya.

Hearing approving laughter, I thought I was on a roll and decided to continue. "See, your tongue is not even suitable for my ass! You better shut up, because your words cause lice to faint and can cause us to lose our jobs!"

The entire group started laughing hysterically and I avoided a dicey situation. Now everyone began joking at Petya's expense. First, of course, was Vanya:

"Listen, Petya, where did you learn such nasty words? Were you a pig farmer before?"

"Petya, why are you not ashamed to say such nasty words? You are a *Komsomolets*[19]! You are embarrassing your last name – Komissarov[20]!"

The education of Komissarov was complete and everyone switched to the regular Russian cursing.

After this episode nobody approached me again with such questions, but I always felt vulnerable. There was an amicable guy among us named Vasya Volokov. He was twenty-two years old. We had a good relationship, helped each other out, and often exchanged the latest news and reminisced about our pasts. Vasya

---

[19] *Komsomolets* - a member of the Komsomol - Young Communist League.
[20] *Commissar* - under the Soviet system, an official of the Communist Party in an army unit. [21]The expression, *Great and Mighty Russian Language*, is taken from Pushkin and is an integral part of the Russian culture and experience.

was very friendly, but I noticed that he systematically kept following me to the toilet making rather flimsy attempts to look at my crotch. I asked him:

"Listen, Vasya, where are you looking at? Are you a homosexual by any chance?"

"What are you talking about? I am not looking anywhere, you are mistaken!"- He answered with visible embarrassment. I knew that I was not mistaken and Vasya stopped following me to the toilet. We continued our friendship.

Despite all my fears, I liked the feeling of being among my own.

The composition of prisoners constantly changed. In the summer of 1942 they brought a civilian named Bogdan. Through hearsay, he had worked for the Germans in a police unit and was sent to the camp for some offense. He was fifty-years old. His whole appearance was revolting - a stocky build, long dangling arms, blinking eyes, and a raspy voice. He resembled a toad. In the evening after work he came a few times to tell us stories about how he had killed Jews in his Ukrainian village. Through him we learned many details about life on the outside.

Bogdan was talkative and retold with great pleasure how in his village the Germans along with the Ukrainian police had massacred Jews. There were peat fields near the village. Peat extraction left deep holes in the ground filled with water. With the participation of local Ukrainians, the Germans gathered all the Jews near the pits and started a show. The Jews were mostly women, children and the elderly, because all the men had been mobilized for the army. The Germans gave rifles to anyone willing to shoot a Jew. With passion and harrowing details Bogdan described how he shot one old man five times, until he fell. "He was a strong Zhid and he was threatening me until I managed to finish him," he noted, matter-of-factly.

"And why did you kill him?"- Someone asked.

"Just for fun," he replied. "Everyone was killing and so did I. The Germans gave each volunteer a glass of vodka."

He thought about this for a moment and added, "Otherwise the Germans would have shot me."

Someone else asked, "Did you also shoot women and children?"

Bogdan stopped for a minute, visibly not knowing what to answer. "No," he said. "I did not, others did. We were all drunk."

It was as if he had been attempting an apology, as much of an apology as could be expected from a drunk.

Bogdan told these stories in a matter-of-fact tone, as if retelling his travel adventures. He told us about the looting of Jewish homes, and then expounded philosophically about how few would survive this war, only the smartest, the strongest and the shrewdest would have a chance (referring of course to himself). Bogdan clearly enjoyed describing executions.

He disappeared from the camp just as quietly as he came into it a few weeks earlier.

These stories weighed heavily on my heart, but I still hoped that my home had not been affected. I had been living for several months among the Germans and had never seen even a hint of the atrocities described by Bogdan.

Perhaps the ancient Roman saying *'Homo homini lupus'* (A man to a man is like a wolf) was intended to insult the wolves. Wolves kill only when hungry. I could not relax even for a moment. I was surrounded by enemies and did not know from which side to expect the most danger.

Another part of my good luck was the fact that we never took a bath or a shower. Most people would disagree, but to me this was the greatest gift possible. Once I got a severe case of scabies. Those who had not suffered from this disease would not understand the extent of my pain and suffering. My entire body had become covered with violently itchy red bumps and any attempt to scratch them immediately led to bloody ulcers. I remember with gratitude my friends who did not betray me to the Germans. If they did I would have been immediately isolated or eliminated. Scabies are very contagious and the Germans were terrified of any infection disease.

From the very beginning I felt that my language was different from my fellow POWs. I used too many urban and intelligent words and, most important, I lacked the wide assortment of curse words which were an integral part of our "Great and Mighty Russian Language"[21]. I could not say that I was totally ignorant, but I obviously was way under par. I urgently needed to address this shortcoming. I ended up being an apt student, and sometimes even wondered, if I ever survived, how I would switch to a normal vocabulary in my future conversations with women and children.

My fellow prisoners were dying in captivity from hunger, cold, diseases and subhuman treatment. This was going on a wide scale basis during the first stages of the war, when the lackluster Soviet leadership brought hundreds of thousands of its soldiers to be captured by the Germans. In 1942-1943, after Stalingrad, the Germans still did not consider Soviet POWs as humans. Even in our relatively 'relaxed' camp, the life of everyone was hanging on a string.

One day, as we led our horses to the river, we passed the gendarmes' house. One POW mounted the horse and galloped to the water. The gendarmes did not like this raucous behavior. Half naked and screaming madly, they ran out of the house, beat him senseless and dragged him into their house. We never saw this prisoner again.

Another six POWs disappeared after saying something about the Soviet Army's success near Moscow. Some fellow prisoners reported this to the Germans and the six POWs were executed as partisans.

In the camp I lost all access to any kind of outside information. There were no newspapers. Except for my master Wilczek, I did not communicate with the Germans. On the other hand, my interaction with fellow prisoners significantly widened my understanding of Soviet life. Most of the POWs were older than I was and had experienced life in reality and not as it was described in newspapers. Most of my life I had lived in a cocoon not really knowing what was going on around me. I learned and remembered a lot, but this newly acquired knowledge did not make my life any easier.

We spent the long winter evenings gathering around a fire in the middle of our mud hut. There was a hole in the ceiling so we would not choke from the smoke. Some dried their clothes, others killed lice. Prisoners liked to sign songs, but their repertoire was quite tragic and depressing:

"Listen my friend, my wounds hurt,

My wounds hurt badly,

One wound is bleeding, another is infected,

The third one will bring me to death."

There were many such songs in Russian folklore for every possible occasion *(in America they would be called The Blues)*. With no cheerful occasions in our life, we did not have any cheerful songs. These songs perfectly described the state of our slowly demoralizing minds, sung to the tune of our constant despair, fear and fatalistic paralysis.

The attitude of the Germans to POWs slowly started changing after Stalingrad, and especially after their defeat near Kursk. We had been taught in school that Karl Marx had said: "The social being determines the consciousness." Karl Marx turned out to be wrong; a more accurate summary would have been "The

Beating determines the consciousness" and everything else for that matter. After the summer of 1943 the random beatings and executions almost ceased. I explain this in part because fewer and fewer Russian soldiers were being captured and more and more Germans found themselves became POWs.

After the war, I often celebrated Victory Day with my friends who had survived the war: Volodya Krizhanovsky, Eugene Vorobyev, Victor Onufriev and many others. Victor came home completely disabled. He fought as a sailor in the Baltic. After the war his ship had been ordered to meet in neutral waters with two barges containing Russian prisoners of war, who the British had passed to the Soviets. When the British tugs disappeared beyond the horizon the order came to torpedo these defenseless barges. Surviving POWs tried to swim and pleaded to Soviet sailors: "What are you doing? We are fellow Russians!" The next order was to shoot the traitors approaching the ship.

Practically, we were doomed. Besides the dangers from either the German or the Soviet captivities, we always had an equal chance of being killed by Russian artillery or bombs. My feelings were ambivalent. Certainly, I was not happy being under Soviet fire, but afterwards I was always pleased to see the Germans nursing their wounds.

In addition to caring for the horses, we transported cargo, moved heavy logs, cleaned the snow off the roads in the winter and mud off the roads in the springtime and restored roadways with sand, rocks and branches.

Once, in the spring of 1942, we were sent on a mission to remove Soviet soldiers killed in an earlier fight. We left before dawn and arrived at our destination just before noon. It was very warm and the Germans were afraid of infections spreading from the decomposing bodies. The German positions were at the top of a hill. The whole 500-600 yards of the hillside was completely covered with bodies of machine-gunned Russian soldiers.

When remembering this field covered with corpses, I often think about the song *This Company* by Vladimir Vysotsky. Obviously, the soldiers had been sent to attack the Germans in waves, motivated by the threat of Soviet machine guns behind. All the bodies were lying in batches, friend under friend.

We placed the corpses on sleds, took them to the other side of the village, dug pits and buried the soldiers. Suddenly we heard the roar of rockets. The Russians were shelling us with their Katyushas[22]. Horses became mad and run in all directions. I hugged the ground trying to survive. The shelling stopped as quickly as it had started. The ground around us was black and covered with fresh shell pits. The air was pierced by an acrid smell of gunpowder. Fortunately, none of the prisoners was hurt. Apparently, the Soviet observers noticed a commotion on the German side and ordered a preemptive strike.

When we returned to the camp, we learned some good news. In our absence, a Soviet rocket had hit a house with twelve

---

[22] *Katyusha* - a Russian truck-mounted mobile rocket launcher, firing salvos of 16-24 rockets with 50 lbs, warheads with a range of about 3-4 miles.

German soldiers. We witnessed their burials. Every soldier was buried in a separate grave with a separate birch cross. I stared at this for a long time - it was poignant and somehow beautiful.

In the summer of 1942, after heavy fighting, the Germans managed to destroy some Russian units and moved the frontline about twenty of twenty-five miles ahead. We were assigned to clear a small stretch of road and fix the bridge that was across a dry riverbed adjacent to the minefield. The Germans were to use our handiwork to force Jewish POWs to run across the minefield, clearing it with human explosions.

That same summer of 1942 saw another escalation of the German advance. We moved closer to the frontline. The Germans set up a 150mm artillery battery right behind our camp. A German surveillance plane, nicknamed 'The Frame' for its twin-boom design, was constantly loitering overhead.

One day we were ordered to harness the horses and wait until further instructions. The Germans had started intensive shelling. A group of dive-bombers dropped their cargo on Russian positions. After the shelling subsided, we were ordered to follow the advancing Germans. We passed the Russian line of defense but did not see any signs of struggle. The trenches were empty – there were no Russian soldiers, living or dead.

After a few hours on the march we heard the sounds of an intense battle ahead. A group of dive bombers flew over our heads toward the frontline. A few minutes later the image that came across the sky looked like it was straight out of a movie. Appearing out of nowhere, Soviet fighters engaged the bombers and were shooting at them down one-by-one. We were barely able to keep count. Some bombers exploded right in the air; others spiraled down with smoke and fire trailing behind them. One bomber, fleeing the Russian fighters, clipped the tops of trees. The whole spectacle lasted only a few minutes, but our joy lasted for a long time. Vanya and I could not reveal our excitement to the Germans and were forced to wait until the end of the day for proper celebration.

By the end of the day, we had reached a small river spanned by a pontoon bridge. The Germans wanted to capture a piece of land near the bridge, but were met with stubborn resistance and barely managed to evacuate the dead and the wounded. Their positions were in clear range of the Russian artillery. The entire riverbank was covered with explosions and smoke. By night, the Germans had retreated. It became clear that the Russians had let the Germans pass their first line of defense and lured them into a trap. It was a bitter lesson for the Germans, who were forced to retreat and build new defense positions from scratch.

The soldiers were dirty and angry and we tried not to attract their attention. When Richter arrived to pick up his horses he muttered, "I have been to Hell!" I hesitated to explore the subject but from later conversations I understood that the Germans had taken heavy casualties.

The Germans dug near the edge of the forest, but later moved deeper in the trees where they built a heavily fortified line of defense: bunkers, anti-tank rails, deep tranches and other fortifications. This line was built by a specialized organization that they called *Todd*, a slave labor unit, using Russian prisoners. The Germans considered these structures to be impenetrable.

Our camp was also moved more deeply into the forest. Horses were put under canopies, guards were put in bunkers and we built barracks for ourselves. It was cold and wet when raining, becoming a little bit warmer after the snow had fallen.

The food shortages continued for weeks. Fodder for the horses was also scarce. With the onset of winter the word Stalingrad was increasingly mentioned. First the newspapers published great success stories of German troops reaching Volga and blocking the main supply artery of the Russian army. As time went by, such stories became rare, replaced with vague articles about the general resilience of the German nation and the courage of the German troops who had broken non-specified Russians blockades. The guards never talked to us about anything except horses. Only Feldwebel Konrad, commander of the horse and POW units tried to tell us something concrete. He even drew a picture in the snow, illustrating how the Russians had surrounded the Germans, who in turn had surrounded the Russians. It was a very elaborate drawing.

Suddenly without any preparation, three-day mourning for the German defeat in Stalingrad had been declared. At the same time Hitler had rather surprisingly promoted his Stalingrad commander, General Freidrich Paulus, to the rank of Field Marshal.

Hitler's theory was no German Field Marshal had ever surrendered in history and he was confident that Paulus would not allow himself to be the first to break that record. Shortly thereafter, General Paulus surrendered himself and his troops to the Russians.

By early winter, we had increasingly started hearing stories about partisans and guerrillas.

Once in the early spring we were ordered to carry logs to the railroad station. The logs were used to build bunkers and fortifications to protect the railroad from the partisans. The German guards looked somewhat strange to us because their uniforms did not fit properly and they had red patches on their sleeves with the letters ROA.

After getting closer we realized that these soldiers were Russians, ROA referring to the Russian Liberation Army. They had privates, sergeants, non-commissioned officers and even a lieutenant. The German lieutenant epaulettes looked very strange paired with the typical Russian peasant face. The lieutenant probably also understood this and quickly disappeared. These 'Germans' used to be ordinary POWs. They told us that their only alternative to joining ROA was death of hunger or cold. Moreover, some of them did not have any warm feelings left toward the Soviet regime. Anybody who had survived the Bolshevik terror, hunger, and life under Communist rule would understand why. We asked the soldiers whether they had killed any partisans. They answered, whether serious or joking I don't know, that they had established a good relationship with the guerillas: they would ask partisans not to bomb the section of the railroad under their protection and everyone was happy.

The ROA soldiers were clearly bothered by their German uniforms, but from what I knew of them, I would not regard them as traitors. They had been betrayed by Stalin, and his cannibalistic policy of rejecting any soldier escaping from occupied territory, encirclement or captivity. Any civilized country would welcome millions of able-bodied soldiers to add to the workforce, but the Soviet regime preferred to give this free labor to the enemy. The ROA soldiers, with rare exceptions, did not shoot fellow Russians. The German command understood this and was busy transferring Russians to the Western front, where they promptly surrendered to the Allies.

A small Russian biplane usually flew over the forest after nightfall. It was called *kukuruznik* (corn fielder) for its small size, silence (often the pilots would turn off its engine) and ability to fly very low. Sometimes the plane would pelt the camp with hand grenades.

From the beginning of the summer of 1943, as soon as the road dried off, the Soviet forces began a big offensive movement. We heard the noise of artillery fire from the north. The noise was so intense that we could not hear individual canon firing, the barrage long since having morphed into a continuous hum. The Germany began leaving their 'impenetrable positions' on the 'streamlined' frontline.

We welcomed the victory of the Russian troops, sharing rumors and news about their success. Each meeting started with the same, "Did you hear about Kharkov?" and "Did you hear about Kursk?" As the Soviet troops advanced, so did the chance that we would encounter SMERSH.

Meanwhile, the Germans fell back to the west at nearly the same speed that they had advanced to the east in 1941. We passed through absolutely devastated villages. All young people had been taken to Germany. At first, the Germans asked for volunteers to work in Germany and even organized several recruitment tours to show the advantages of the German way of life. The volunteers soon realized that they were facing slavery and started hiding from recruiters. The volunteerism ended very quickly and slave hunting began. In one village a girl had escaped from the recruiters and hid in a haystack. First the Germans thrust the haystack with bayonets and afterwards set it on fire.

Retreating Germans destroyed bridges, railway tracks and anything else that could be used by the advancing Soviet troops. The soldiers started spreading rumors of new wonder weapons, tanks, missiles and aircraft. These were expected to lead Germany to victory. They talked about a super-bomb which would freeze all life within several miles around the explosion. These rumors were supposed to compensate for the retreat and lift the sagging morale of the troops.

The Germans would stop and take up defensive positions only to abandon them a few days later and move further west. As we entered Belarus, we started increasingly seeing gallows. The hung by the Germans people had attached signs with a word 'Partisan'.

Once, approaching a small village, I saw scattered pieces of book pages alongside the road. My heart sunk. Those were Jewish books. The closer we came to the village the more books I saw on the ground. The pages were not yellow and there was no evidence of long-term exposure to weather. Whatever happened must have happened very recently. I remembered Bogdan's stories and realized what had transpired. It did not matter whether the Jews were killed right there or were taken to other places to be massacred – the destroyed Jewish books screamed about their tragedy.

I was consumed with rage, frustration, helplessness, hate, empathy, and compassion toward my fellow Jews. I feared that I might be unable to restrain myself and alert my captors to the fact that I was a Jew. German soldiers did not talk about it. Perhaps they may have condoned what happened or maybe they were too afraid to speak out. I noticed that the Germans criticized their commanders and expressed dissident thoughts rather freely, especially compared with the Soviet soldiers, but that license had its limits. They would never discuss the policy toward Jews.

When we entered the village it was already dark and we did not see any traces of the pogrom. Next to the watering hole I saw several Germans talking with one of the residents in what sounded like Yiddish. The civilian was a typical Jew – tall, slim, dark-haired, with a thick black beard. When our eyes had met, I froze, realizing that he had discovered me. This was not such a difficult task, particularly for another Jew. My dress differed from the German and the other POWs' uniforms and, well, because I thought I looked like a Jew. When I took the horses away from the well, the tall Jew turned around and looked at me again. Later Wilczek told me that that the man who I thought was a typical Jew was in fact the village chief, and that they spoke in the Swabian dialect of German (I still maintain it was Yiddish), which Wilczek had learned during the First World War while being held as a German prisoner.

At the beginning of the war the Russian troops were continuously retreating and any and all offensive initiative was completely on the side of the Germans. The balance flipped in 1943 and by 1944 the initiative had passed to the Russians. The war had moved into a new phase.

In the fall, the Germans crossed the Dnepr River, took up positions on the high western river bank and built very impressive fortifications. The fortifications were considered to be impenetrable and they really looked like they might actually *be* impenetrable. We were put in stables on former cow farm about fifteen miles from the frontline. There was almost no food. We were given sickles and ordered to cut the grass and feed the horses. The sickle looked to me like a very simple tool, but without prior experience I could not make it work. Vanya's help saved me. We brought the hay back and got some food to eat. For two days I was walking bent at the waist.

The Germans did not have time to dig in on new positions. The shelling started right away. Unlike during past years, this time the Soviet artillery was much more accurate and the Germans took heavy casualties. To replenish their ranks the Germans began to bring Yugoslavs and Turks, who spoke neither German nor Polish and were impossible to understand. The Germans were good at inventing ersatz-oil, ersatz-soap, and ersatz-coffee. Now they made ersatz-soldiers. By all the indicators a *kaput* was coming, this time it was a real one, not an ersatz.

One day in June 1944, we were ordered to harness our horses and follow the infantry. We were walking all night under a full moon. By early morning we reached some small village and made camp. Throughout the night we listened to the intensive firefights surrounding us. At dawn, suddenly was awakened by a hum from above. I looked at the sky and counted eighteen two-engined silver airplanes, each sparkling like child's toy under the morning sun. Peering upward, I made out a few black spots, slowly separating from these 'toys' and tumbling to the earth. I realized they were bombs and barely had time to warn Vanya. We ducked in a small trench nearby. The bombing ended quickly. A crater from an exploded bomb was smoking right next to our trench. We were stunned to find ourselves alive and gathered our spooked horses and continued our march. After three hours of walking I felt some discomfort on my left side – something was scratching my ribs. I looked under my shirt and found a small, shiny metal piece, the size of a match head, lodged under my rib. I pulled it out and threw it away. I still have a small scar on my flank as a war souvenir.

We barely had time to reach the forest before a new batch of low-flying aircraft arrived. Vanya and I promptly hit the ground playing our usual game: "Will it hit or will it not?" When the bombing ended, I saw a bomb crater, just twenty inches from my left foot. We got up, cleaned ourselves off and were immediately shocked by a huge explosion, just a few yards from us. It was a delayed charge bomb. The explosion produced a huge crater, nine or ten feet in diameter and several feet deep. It was our luck that the delayed charge bomb had dug rather deep under the ground before exploding. The soil dampened the force of the explosion and prevented shrapnel from killing everyone around.

Without any time to count our blessings, immediately after the explosion we heard machine gun fire. It was coming from the returning aircraft. We jumped into a fresh bomb crater and found it full of other people covered in dirt – we could not even tell whether they were German soldiers or POWs, but at the moment, it did not matter. After waiting for a while we cautiously climbed back. Vanya noticed that my left leg was bloody. Initially I did not feel the pain. Perhaps it was the shrapnel from the delayed charge bomb which finally got me. Then I also noticed that Vanya's sleeve was covered in blood. He was wounded in his right shoulder.

The shelling and the explosion and the machine gun chatter continued for barely fifteen minutes but in my memories of these events it seemed like an eternity.

We got back to the road but could not find our convoy. The hundreds of carts, soldiers, horses and military equipment that had been marching on the same road just fifteen minutes earlier had not left a trace. There were no bomb craters, no wounded horses, and no abandoned broken equipment. We heard machine gun fire right behind us and decided to move in the opposite direction. The road was empty. After a while, we saw an approaching truck with three soldiers and boxes of ammunition. Suspiciously looking at us and our uniform, they stopped us for questioning. We did not have any papers except our 'Property of The Army' armbands. Our wounds probably saved us this time around.

I told them that our position was bombed and attacked by Russian tanks which penetrated the German defense. I lied about tanks just to scare the Germans. Maybe I spoke too eloquently, and so the German sergeant ordered us into the truck. They turned it around and went back in the direction the truck had come from. After thirty minutes we reached what used to be a large village. It was now a collection of burned buildings, thanks to a good job by the Russian air force. The German stopped the truck and sent us to the field hospital.

A newly built road led to the hospital. In one of the trenches on the side of the road, we saw a wounded German soldier. His jacket and trousers were completely laced through by shrapnel. A blood trail of about fifteen foot indicated that he probably had tried to reach the edge of the road and ask for help, but did not have strength to do so. The soldier looked at us and there was no fear or pain in his eyes - just doom. Somehow, we felt compassion for this poor guy.

The field hospital was located in a huge specially equipped mud hut. The room was very dim with a few carbide lamps. A nurse looked at my leg and yelled, *"Bombenspliter im linken Oberschenkel!"* (A fragment in the upper thigh!) and sent me to the next office. Another nurse gave me a tetanus shot and cleaned my wounds. The third one wrote my name, attached a red label to my jacket and sent me to an adjacent room with benches occupied by injured soldiers. I dared not lie down. I could not sit either, more so from the tetanus shot than from my wounds. So I was left standing in the corner waiting for what would happen next. Vanya got a different color label and was sent to another room. We did not see each other ever again. I was eternally sorry to part with such a dear friend.

Because of the darkness the nurse probably did not see my 'Property of The Army' band and did not recognize my foreign uniform. On his question "Was hast du?" ('What do you have?'), I answered, *"Bombenspliter im linken Oberschenkel."* He probably mistook me for a German and sent me to the medical unit for regular soldiers.

The room was full of wounded soldiers who I did not recognize. I tried not to speak and responded to all inquiries with one phrase, *"Bombenspliter im linken Oberschenkel."* I did not dare to take off my armband since it was my only ID, but I covered the armband with mud. I was not quite sure why I decided to do this, but figured it would attract less attention.

We got into covered trucks and rode for a very long time. During our journey the convoy was bombed several times. After reaching a railway station we were transferred to train cars. I was very tired and did not speak to anyone. I sat quietly with my eyes closed and portrayed terrible suffering. My behind really *was* hurting. Furthermore, my left ankle started to hurt also. When I took off my boot I found a small shell fragment. Half of it had lodged under my skin, right below the bone. The other half was blatantly shining at me like a bright piece of jewelry. I easily pulled it out.

No one paid attention to my strange uniform. They had more important things to worry about. We were given something to eat and a pack of cigarettes. I ate my food but gave away the cigarettes and immediately became everyone's favorite. As we were preparing to leave, a brief stint of rifle fire showered our train. Soldiers joked that it was the 'partisans' farewell'.

I settled on the top shelf and looking out the window tried to understand where I was going. On one hand, I thought it was better to be as far away from the SMERSH as possible; on the other hand I was afraid of the unknown.

Finally the train left and the mood of the soldiers clearly lifted. Each of them was looking forward to hopefully seeing their friends and relatives in Germany. My head was soft from the exhaustion and my heart heavy at not knowing when I would have the same hopeful feelings of seeing my friends and family. We found out that the train would first stop in Warsaw and everyone would be forced to pass a health inspection for venereal diseases.

When I heard this, I realized that after all the trials that I had been through this health inspection would certainly be my death sentence.

15. PURGATORY

Slowly like a turtle and as inevitable as fate, the train carried me forward.

I vividly imagined myself arriving at a sanitary checkpoint in Warsaw. I saw myself being dragged to a medical examination and being ordered to undress. This was the end of my thoughts. Like game cornered by a hunter, I could not think about what would happen next.

In my respite, I watched with great delight the convoys of tanks, guns and soldiers rushing to the east. Judging by the quantity and size of the convoys, the Germans were in great need of cannon fodder to patch their defenses punctured by the Russians.

Next morning our train stopped near a barracks in a suburb of Warsaw. All walking patients were counted on the ramp and transferred to one of the barracks. Seriously wounded soldiers in groups of thirty men were carried to another barrack for a medical checkup and initial treatment. It was a well organized flow which was rigidly enforced under the German overarching principle of *ordung* (order).

My turn came within a couple of hours. Everyone was given a numbered sack to put their clothes in before going to the shower room. I tried to be the last in the showers. It was a large room filled with about thirty men sharing about twenty showerheads. The room was filled with steam. Having gone without showering for months, people became ecstatic, yelling, screaming and singing from pleasure. I hid in the corner behind some other guy - trying to wash myself and be invisible at the same time.

Thanks to the heavy steam I managed to stay unexposed. Once I got to the next room I grabbed a towel as fast as I could, but my luck did not last for very long. Just like in a factory conveyer, we marched through the narrow corridor towards two elderly soldiers, who held big brushes covered with smelly liquid. At the end of the corridor everyone dropped their towels, lifted their hands up and these two soldiers covered our hairy areas with this liquid - under the armpits and in the groins.

This was done very quickly and efficiently. The liquid smelled terribly and irritated everyone's eyes and skin. The first soldier brushed under my arms and I was relieved that he was not looking down. I hesitated, not daring to move forward to the second soldier. This delayed the whole conveyer; I got a strong push from behind and ended up right in front of the second soldier. I frantically waved my hands around trying to cover up my crotch, expecting the imminent cry, "Look, I found a Jew!" But nothing happened. The old soldier brushed me with his skunky liquid, rather indifferently, without even looking. Not realizing that the danger was over, I was pushed to another room where I found my disinfected belongings in the numbered sack.

The whole procedure: stripping, showers, brushing, and dressing lasted approximately thirty or forty minutes, but it seemed to me like a whole eternity, which, I might suppose, the proper Purgatory *meant* to feel like.

Again, I remained alive.

Someone may find such frequent and detailed descriptions of experiences like those above to be abnormal or paranoid, but after the antisemitism of my childhood, after the endless hysterical anti-Jewish howl in German newspapers, after the terrifying stories I had heard in the POW camp and after the massacred Jewish villages I had seen during the endless march, I had developed an acute self-defense reflex for any potential antisemitic threat. I was prepared for any threat, real or perceived, expecting it from every German I met. Until this day I still carry this reflex with me.

Once dressed, I proceeded to another room where they treated and bandaged my wounds. It was very painful, but I did not feel any pain. I was giddy and ecstatic and still not entirely convinced that I had escaped again.

We were housed in a three-story former school building in the center of Warsaw. The classrooms had been converted to hospital wards. Once we took our respective beds, the soldiers began a meaningless bunter. I recognized several soldiers with whom I had taken the shower a couple of hours ago. Suddenly, the conversation switched to the topic of circumcision. A young soldier who had stood next to me during the disinfection procedure started the discussion.

For obvious reasons I thought that I had been detected. Possibly this was the case, but the conversation remained very abstract, without naming names or pointing in my direction. Naturally, the talk started with the Jews, but it was not in the usual hateful tone of the propaganda printed in newspapers. The soldiers discussed that Jews very intelligently circumcise their children at an early age and in a very hygienic manner. My next bed neighbor said that he had been circumcised at the age of eight for medical reasons and still remembered how painful it was. I was really glad to hear this, but shut up and stayed quiet pretending that this topic had nothing to do with me.

From the topic of circumcision we moved on to other Jewish topics. The old-time patients reported about the Warsaw Ghetto uprising and how the Jews had fought ferociously, often using the weapons which some Germans had sold in exchange for jewelry. Nobody spoke about the mass extermination of innocent people, mostly of women and children.

So far my strange uniform did not raise anyone's suspicion. After a while I lost my vigilance. It was very hot and my next bed neighbor, who was about my age, offered to go out and get some fresh air. Crowds of wounded soldiers loitered in the courtyard. Suddenly I heard a call. "Roman, what you are doing here?" I looked around and saw Wenzel, one of the soldiers I knew from before.

If I were asked to name the person who I would want to have seen at that moment the least, Polachek would be first and his friend Wenzel would be a close second. The rest of German soldiers had treated us for the most part with complete indifference, except for Polachek and Wenzel who had always looked at me with poorly concealed threat.

Wenzel was originally from Alsace, and in my understanding he was a Frenchman, since Alsace was part of France before 1872 and from 1918 until 1940. The idea that a Frenchman would treat me with such malice was particularly unpleasant to me.

"What are you doing here?" he asked again. His look did not bode well.

I told him about the bombing and wounding. While I spoke, he looked at me as a cobra at a rabbit. I felt like he was deciding whether to check his suspicions that I was a Jew by himself or report it to superiors.

I tried to break his thoughts and with great involvement asked about what had happened to him, Polachek and Richter. How his wound was healing? Was he receiving treatment? He told me that Polachek had been killed by the Russians, and I made such a face that he decided I was about to cry. I never suspected I had such great artistic abilities.

As the conversation progressed, I noticed his tension subsiding. He told me that the Russians with heavy tanks and artillery went on the offensive. He was shot in the shoulder very early during the battle and managed to reach the field hospital. He did not see Richter but doubted anyone could have survived such heavy fire.

Under the pretext that I had a scheduled procedure, I ended the conversation and went inside. I felt great relief when I later learned that Wenzel was sent to another hospital.

16. IN AUSTRIA

After two days I was sent to a hospital in Austria along a small group of soldiers. Despite their wounds, the soldiers were in a very good mood hoping to visit their homes. Since the initial checkup, my wound did not get any medical care and it began to pulsate with pain. It was very uncomfortable to sit.

Eventually we arrived in Bad Goisern, located near the town of Linz (Mozart's birthplace). It was raining. We were greeted by two nurses from the hospital. They complained that the hospital had no automobiles and we had to walk from the station to the hospital. I had trouble understanding their dialect. Because of the rain we lost our way and arrived at the hospital when it was already dark. For some reason the whole floor smelled extremely unpleasant – probably the sewage was broken. We were very pleased to be given hospital pajamas and to be directed towards showers with separate stalls!

Afterward we were given a medical checkup. The nurse took my bandage off, did not like what she saw and called for a senior nurse. They discussed whether they would have to open the wound and finally decided to wait until the doctor arrived next day. I was taken to a small room and assigned a bed. There was no food: the kitchen was closed.

The next morning I woke up to bright sunlight. All the patients were still asleep and I decided to go outside. Once I got out I froze in amazement.

So far, the most beautiful vistas I had ever seen in my life were of the Kiev parks above the Dnepr River and of my village, where I had spent my first ten years. Sentimental feelings aside, my village left some indelible footprints in my mind: the stunning purity of the lake, the gorgeous estate of former sugar baron Tereshchenko, the forest of huge centuries-old oaks and chestnuts, and the exquisite mansion built by French architects, all of them set like jewels in the diadem of the splendid Ukrainian countryside. I was lucky to have seen all of it and have such vivid memories of it semi-intact, before, as they sang in the Russian version of *L' Internationale*[23]: "We shell destroy the old world to its foundation!"

But nothing compared with the beauty I saw that moment in Bad Goisern. I looked at the huge, almost imposing, mountains with their jagged peaks. Their grim grandeur was mesmerizing. It was mid-summer, but their peaks were covered with snow. There was a hut attached to a rock near the summit. It was hard to imagine how people could reach such heights.

Our hospital stood in the middle of a scenic meadow, among flowers, trees and neatly manicured grass. For a moment I forgot where I was. When I returned to the house I was brought back to reality. The outside splendor clashed sharply with the

---

[23] *L' Internationale* – a song of French origin, written in the late 19th century in the Paris commune that later became the anthem for international socialism. It served as the national anthem for the Soviet Union until after WWII.

dilapidated interior. Breakfast would consist of a thin slice of bread slightly covered with margarine and cup of flower tea.

The newly arrived soldiers were indignant and complained, "Aren't they ashamed to put such a small piece of bread on such a large plate?"

Those who stayed longer quickly would calm the newbie down. "It is because of your arrival that we got an extra treat. Usually we don't see such abundance."

"Drink more tea – it fills the stomach very well."

"They (the hospital staff) make you want to return to the frontline quicker!"

After all these jokes the recovering soldiers would describe the food shortages among the civilian population. They told us about cases of theft and murder caused by food disputes, unheard of before the war in Austria notable for its law-abiding citizenry. Such talks continued, in different variations, on a daily basis.

The scarce rationing extended to everything, including clothing. My blue pants were full of holes. While providing excellent ventilation, they may have offended the aesthetic senses of people around me. I did not worry much, because I had no money, no rationing vouchers and walked exclusively in hospital pajamas. The pajamas had provided me with a much needed cover. Nobody knew who I was.

After breakfast I was called to the examination room and ordered to lay flat on my stomach and bare my buttocks. I completed the order with no hesitation - there were no signs of my nationality on my ass. The doctor took his time picking the shell fragments out of my wound. As a substitute for anesthesia, a good looking nurse periodically slapped the other half of my buttocks. It was more painful than pleasurable, but I did not scream, purely out of politeness – the girl was trying very hard.

Afterwards I barely reached my bed and fell asleep. A neighbor woke me up for lunch. All the meals in the hospital were a good illustration for the German slogan: 'Guns Instead of Butter'. I used to be hungry, but because I was always busy I did not have time to think about food. There was nothing else to do in the hospital but to start thinking about lunch immediately after breakfast.

In the evening I was able to briefly walk in the garden, alight with fireflies. I had never seen so many fireflies before; the whole area looked like fireworks. After a few days the fireflies disappeared.

I learned that the hospital was rebuilt from a convalescent hotel for patients with arthritis, rheumatism and similar diseases. It was situated on top of a sulfur spring, which explained the unpleasant smell that hit me the first day. There was a bathhouse in the basement and occasionally I saw patients brought there in wheelchairs for treatment.

A few days later a nurse told me that I was ordered to work for an Austrian to help with cleaning, heating and other menial jobs. The girl was obviously embarrassed telling me this, and quickly added that I must come back regularly for medical procedures. I knew my place and I had been expecting such an order. I was touched by the girl's embarrassment, but I was not certain that she understood why I was singled out among the rest.

After the last three weeks of mortal danger the hospital was like a God's gift to me. The sense of anxiety never left, but I was able to relax somewhat. My hospital pajamas definitely helped me to blend in. Moreover, it was an Austrian hospital and the Austrians had not been Nazified completely yet. I observed some tensions between the Austrians and the Germans. Once, when the soup was particularly thin, one of the Germans said:

"I understand that this is wartime, but such swill will do me in, saving Russians some ammunition."

A women cook replied crying, "This is not my war! I did not start it. My children would be happy to get such soup."

There were very few newspapers but even the ones we had nobody read. The newspapers reported the same thing - soldiers fighting valiantly, the *Wehrmacht* taking new impenetrable positions and the accumulation of resources for an overwhelming strike. There was increased talk about new secret weapons, which would decide the outcome of the war.

One of the newspapers, I think it was *Frankfurter Allgemeine*, drew my attention. One article read that a Jewish battalion formed in Palestine was fighting SS troops in Italy as part of a British division. Both sides took heavy casualties. This was a very unusual article for a German newspaper. I kept this article for a long time and regretted that I had nobody to share it with.

During one weekend all walking patients were ordered to go to church for a meeting. Some local Fuhrer was the speaker. He repeated the boring nonsense written every day in newspapers and soldiers slowly began to sneak out from the church. I remembered only one thing – an outrage about some ignorant German soldiers engaging in sexual relationships with Russians women, increasing the quality of the enemy's breeding stock.

I noticed that the same German soldiers without uniforms and weapons became much friendlier. I felt that my next bed neighbor, who was about my age, sympathized with me. Such nuances are difficult to describe, but he always called me for a walk when I was free, waited for me to go for a meal and helped with other small things.

I quickly found a common ground with the Austrian to whom I was assigned and hit it off, especially with his horse. During our talks the Austrian mostly reminisced about how well they lived before the war, and how good this hotel had been before. I listened to him attentively and was careful not to ask any questions, trying to understand his dialect.

His name was Karl. He was very old. He wore leather shorts and a crude jacket. His horse was a comparable age. When the road was going uphill the horse would stop. This meant that the horse needed a rest and some help. Karl and I would help by pushing the cart uphill and the three of us would somehow manage to get over the incline.

When I told Karl my name he asked, "Are you from Bukovina?"

I answered, "Almost. I am from Kiev."

Since 1939 Bukovina had been a part of Ukraine, but between the wars it was a part of Romania and before the WW1 it had belonged to the Austro-Hungarian Empire. Ukrainians who lived in the province were considered to be Austrians. Karl hardly knew where Kiev was, but my answer left him satisfied.

Karl was very hard working, but his age and the constant hunger affected his strength. He would run out of breath after a steep climb and would stand for a while with his eyes closed, catching his breath. We had to clean the territory, remove debris and carry food, coal and other staples. Thanks to these errands I was able to see this village.

It was hard to tell if it was a town or a village and what the locals did for a living. The houses, small and beautiful, looked like they had come from a toy factory.

I tried to help Karl as much as I could. I nurtured the idea that my superiors would appreciate my hard work and keep me at the hospital. I was here by mistake, but I hoped that my free labor was well worth a little bit of extra food to the hospital. Alas, the German system worked like a clock and after a few weeks it spat me out.

A soldier escorted me to Vienna. The train station had survived, but the adjacent railway tracks were completely destroyed. The Americans considered Austria to be occupied by the

Germans, and therefore bombed only military objects. Not a single bomb hit the city or the buildings occupied by civilians.

The soldier brought me to some agency, got a receipt and left. Overnight I was sent to a barracks, where I met another Russian POW. Our guard was so old that he was probably conscripted during the Franco-German war of 1871. He barely moved his legs and probably could not lift his rifle, dragging it along with his gas mask behind him.

The next day my journey to the West began. It was so rapid and with so many stops along the way, that the details blurred together into a dreamlike state.

17. FRANCE FROM BEHIND THE BARS

Once we climbed into the cars we heard our guards calling out our destination –it was Strasbourg. In the morning we crossed the former Austro-German border into Germany proper. The allied air raids occurred every couple hours. Our train hid from the raids underground, in the tunnels. Large groups of thirty of forty American B-17 Flying Fortress bombers periodically dropped bright strips of aluminum paper to confuse German radars and continued flying deeper into Germany towards their next target. Looking out from the train we clearly saw the extent of the devastation the Nazis had brought onto their country. Many cities had been completely destroyed by American bombing.

We arrived in Strasbourg at night. Before 1940 this used to be France. We did not see the city, but noticed cleanliness, an array of flowers planted around the station and the tram track neatly lowered in the asphalt to allow for smooth car traffic.

Our next stop was Belfort. Again, we arrived in the morning, and were ordered to get out and march up the mountain along the twisty cobble road. Apparently, Belfort used to be a fortress several hundred years ago. On the right side of the road stood a tall three-story fortress wall adorned with various medieval architectural features; such as windows, crenellations, and embrasures.

The climb was very steep. Our elderly guard barely moved his feet. We offered to help and without hesitation he dropped all of his belongings on us, including his rifle. I told him that we would return the rifle, but only if he brought us to a place with food. He did not care.

On the way up we passed two Frenchmen engaged in a lively conversation. Suddenly, one of them turned back and in perfect Russian asked us who were we. We introduced ourselves and explained our situation. He told us about a camp for Russian prisoners of war being built nearby. He came to France after the revolution, and today was his special day: his daughter was marrying a Frenchman. He pointed to the beaming groom standing next to him. Initially our Soviet mentality triggered an alert: "Be careful, He is a white counterrevolutionary!" but we quickly calmed down and appreciated speaking with someone in our native tongue.

At the top of the hill was the entrance to the city, guarded by two German soldiers. Before presenting our credentials, our almost senile gray haired guard started cleaning himself up to look more presentable. We joked that he really did not need to try because he looked so good already that he would immediately be sent to the Eastern front. He smiled and replied that he would only qualify for the *Inner Dienst* (The Domestic Service).

The German army had large Yugoslav, Arab and Indian contingents. They sported German uniforms with exotic accessories in the form of turbans and fez hats and their look would no doubt make any Parisian haute couture fashion show. They did not understand a single word of German.

All recent news were pointing to an upcoming *kaput* for Hitler's Germany. Moreover, a new tone had penetrated the newspapers. One paper wrote that the opening of the Western front had put the Soviets into a terrible situation. Another one wrote that the Soviet army was incapacitated, virtually exhausted, and that the American troops would soon join the Germans to deliver an overwhelmingly blow to the Soviets. The German propaganda had increasingly become hysterical and plain crazy, but the Germans obediently consumed all this nonsense. It was apparent that the war was lost, but the army machine could not stop and continued the usual routine.

The prison camp was located at the end of the railway tracks and consisted of several railway cars, about forty people in each. I was separated from a fellow POW traveler and put in a different car. Most prisoners there were Russian and Ukrainian, as well as two Poles and some Kazakhs who had worked on German factories. Some had bandages and were nursing their wounds. The following morning a locomotive hooked up our cars and began dragging us to some god forsaken place nobody knew.

I tried to understand the direction of our travel, but the French station signs were meaningless to me. All that I remember were the names of a few stations: Lyon, Dijon, Macon. We stopped in Macon. The security around our cars had increased. The cars were locked for 24 hours and we were given food and water through thick metal bars. At the stops we were escorted to toilets.

Judging by their tattoos, speech and behavior, the guards were conscripted from local criminals. They did not fuss with us and never hesitated to deliver kicks and blows for any reason or without a reason. They reminded me of the Ukrainian policemen during October-November of 1941.

The camp was originally intended to house slave laborers working on defense fortifications against the advancing Americans. The rapid Allied movement put these plans in disarray and the Germans did not know what to do with us. I heard a conversation between two guards, "... Just shoot these pieces of shit and let's go home before it's too late...." Another voice replied, "... but would not we be executed ourselves?" I had no doubt they were talking about us.

For several days my wound was getting worse and worse. I was not able to see my behind, but felt a growing inflammation there by touch. Complaining to the authorities would be very dangerous. One of the prisoners, a former paramedic, looked at my wound and told me that the only solution would be to drain the pus from the abscess. I had no choice but agree to this procedure and obediently bent over the stool. I felt the guy doing something to me and suddenly darkness enveloped my world. I heard a voice from afar and then fainted. I came back to a mug of water being poured on my head.

"All right," said my doctor. "I squeezed the pus out. Relax and keep your behind exposed until the wound is dry and you will be fine. Now you have a spare hole in your ass."

One day, when we were still staying in Macon, two POWs from each car were taken to a riverbank. Several mutilated corpses laid near the river. The camp commandant claimed that these people were prisoners who escaped from the camp, got intercepted by the French Resistance and were brutally murdered. This was clearly a lie, since nobody could identify the dead. Most likely the Germans had killed some random folk and tried to scare us from ever thinking about escaping.

The situation in the German army was rapidly deteriorating. Soviet troops reached Vistula and waited until the Germans brutally suppressed the Warsaw rebellion. The Polish organizers of the rebellion were objectionable to Stalin because they were loyal not to him, but to the exiled Polish government in London. The Allies gained strength and expanded the offensive. The German soldiers increasingly preferred to surrender to the Americans, rather than fighting futile battles. The huge numbers of American flying fortresses made the skies look like rush hour in a large city.

Our train went further east and until we stopped near the city of Milhauzen. This former French city, along with Strasbourg and the rest of Alsace and Lorraine, was declared a part of Germany after the French defeat in 1940. We were put in a warehouse on the outskirts of the city. Every day the guards selected a group of two to five prisoners and took them somewhere. This was a clearly an ominous sign and in our experience, this likely meant an execution. Who knew what could come to the mind of the dying Nazis?

18. IN GERMANY

Suddenly, we found out that our regular guards had disappeared and only the local police remained. From the camp population they selected a group of eighteen or twenty people, organized us in two columns and marched us to the east. Initially the guards refused to answer where we were going. After a while we reached a river. Immediately we were told that it was the Rhine and they were going to hand us over to civilian authorities.

We crossed the Rhine over a lightweight wooden bridge and for the first time ended up on proper German soil. I had imagined the Rhine to be a wide, calm, navigable river, but we saw a powerful roaring stream, hugged by high and rocky banks. The roar was so strong that I could not hear my neighbor. The German side, as far as my eyes could see, was completely covered with concrete reinforcements. This was, as we found out later, the 'Siegfried Line' constructed against the French 'Maginot Line'. When the Germans occupied France they immediately blew up the 'Maginot Line'. In turn the Allies immediately blew up the ''Siegfried Line' after the German defeat.

After marching for several miles we reached the village of Weisweil. This was a big village, stretched out along the river within half a mile from the riverbank. Later I understood why there

139

were no buildings near the river – it was a no-man's land, a part of the 'Siegfried Line'.

The policeman checked every name against the list and passed us to the village Mayor. As agricultural workers, we were at the complete disposal of local farmers. We were given blue *OST* patches, and were warned never to appear outside without them. We became a type of slaves called *Ostarbeiters*.

We waited outside the city to be picked up by our new masters. The Mayor noticed bandages under some prisoners' clothing. He suspiciously asked if anyone was injured or somewhat disabled. In such cases, he said, the doctor would be available here the next morning.

My new master came after noon. She gave me a hostile look and asked what I could do. I said that I could do everything – I could tend horses and cows, mow grass, help with housework and added that I had lived in a village and was accustomed to hard peasant labor.

"Can you milk cows?" she asked.

"Of course. My family had a cow and I used to milk her," I replied.

It was a half-lie; we had had a cow, but after my Mom died all my attempts to milk it were useless – the cow just ran away and gave no milk.

My wound was wet and just in case I asked my owner if she would allow me to see a doctor the next morning. She asked suspiciously, "You cannot work? Are you wounded?"

I was afraid to be sent back and quickly assured her, "No, no, I can work just fine. After my injury I worked in a hospital. I just need to change my bandages and it would be better done by a doctor, but if you object, I can do it perfectly well myself. I am merely following the Mayor's instructions about the doctor." I also added my trusted phrase: *"Bombenspliter im linken Oberschenkel."*

She ordered me to walk back and forth to make sure she had not received damaged goods. She liked what she saw, said "Gut" and allowed me to go visit the doctor.

We came to a large two-story house. I was ordered to go to the kitchen. There were two other laborers: a very unfriendly Pole about twenty-five years old, called Stas, and a Russian girl from Leningrad. Her name was Lena and she was a student when she was captured by the Germans on the outskirts of Leningrad in 1941 while digging anti-tank trenches. After lunch the caretaker of the house, Frau Anna, told me to work with Stas and follow his instructions.

I visited the doctor in the morning. He was a very old man, half blind. I told him about my *"Bombenspliter im linken Oberschenkel"*. He examined the wound, put some ointment, changed the bandages and said that everything was OK.

The next morning I received a surprise - an order to be checked for venereal diseases. According to German laws, everyone coming from France was required to undergo such testing. For obvious reasons I did not like this law. I told my master that I had just visited the doctor and she may call the registration room to verify. She called and indeed found name in the doctor's visitation book. I had dodged the bullet yet again.

I started working for Stas. From the very beginning I felt his hostility toward me. He always assigned the hardest and dirtiest jobs to me. He also complained to my owner that I did not know how to milk cows. He did it in broken German supplemented with plenty of hand gestures. I explained that I needed a few days to practice. The Frau agreed and even smiled. When Stas saw her reply he became green with anger. Later I realized that the main reason why he hated me was my friendly relations with Lena.

Lena was a very cute and smart girl, about twenty-two years old. She was a student at the university, majoring in Russian language and literature and preparing to become a teacher in high school. She loved literature and we continuously discussed the books which we both read and many other topics of common interest. Our discussions usually took place in the evenings after work, in the kitchen. Stas never missed our conversations. He did not understand Russian but was afraid to leave us alone even for a minute. By ten o'clock he would start to swear *"Psya krev, cholera"*. He really wanted to sleep, but would not leave.

I think he loved Lena. She was hard not to love. She was glowing with kindness and affection. Even the Frau respected her. We were just very good friends sharing a common past. Stas became increasingly irritated and angry at our conversations and Lena's good attitude toward me. There could not be any reasons for this other than jealousy.

For some people hate trumps all other human feelings, and Stas was one of them. His hate caught up with me many years after the war had ended.

It was in 1960, fifteen years after the war. I had already been exonerated and no longer was considered to be 'the enemy of the people'. I had a decent job, a passport and held permanent residency in Kiev (which was a big deal at that time). I had even received a medal for 'Participation in the Great Patriotic War'. I was quite surprised when out of nowhere I received a warrant to appear in the OBHSS (department of economic crimes) office in the Ministry of Internal Affairs.

Everyone knew that when called to the OBHSS one should prepare some bread and a change of clean clothing, just in case. I always remembered a Soviet saying, "If a person exists, the case can always be invented."

At the appointed time I was in the ministry building. I was met by a person in civilian clothes who introduced himself as a NKVD lieutenant. The OBHSS warrant was just a cover, so that I 'would not worry in advance'. He was investigating a letter (he did not specify the contents of the letter) and asked me to retell the story of my captivity. Throughout the post-war years I had told this story countless times to different investigators in Filtration NKVD camps in Germany, SMERSH units in the Army, the Ministry of Internal Affairs in Kiev, and many others. I repeated it again. He carefully listened and asked if I knew a man called Wojciechowski. I said that I was not sure, but probably it was a Pole, with whom I

143

had been in captivity in the village of Weisweil in Germany. I did not know his last name, but his first name was Stas and there also was a girl from Leningrad called Lena. The investigator said that Stas had written a letter about me to the NKVD, which triggered this investigation. The lieutenant said that he still had no authority to tell me the contents of the letter, but I should not worry and could go.

I cannot imagine what Stas had written in the letter. There was no romantic relationship between Lena and me. She was a pure and serious girl, too good for a meaningless war romance.

Throughout the war, it appeared as though I did not have much luck with Poles (Polachek, Wilczek, Stas, Polish–French soldiers). Even after our liberation, on our way home through Poland, the Poles showered us, ex-prisoners, with stones.

After the war I did, however, befriend a Pole, Volodya Krzhizhanovsky. We maintained a very long family friendship and spent many holidays together until my emigration.

I was spared from milking cows mainly because along with other prisoners I was constantly pulled to higher priority assignments such as clearing bunkers on the Siegfried Line, digging trenches, and building anti-tank fortifications.

After a while the Frau got used to me and even started talking to me. She complained about the lack of letters from her husband and showed me his photo. A quite elderly man stared back at me from the card. Frau Anna looked much younger than her husband. They had one five-year-old daughter. Their farm was rather large - ten cows, two horses, three laborers (us) and a huge apple orchard between the village and the Rhine. The orchard required a lot of work, especially in the fall when we had to squeeze the juice from the apples. The Frau received very limited supplies of sugar from the authorities and under her strict supervision we poured the juice into the barrels and added sugar.

In December we got Christmas greetings from Russia – snow fell for several days. The Germans made a desperate counter-attack attempt in the north of Belgium, near the Ardennes. Those were clearly the last convulsions, but the newspapers screamed constantly about the 'Invincible German Army' even after the attack fizzled and the Allies moved in.

In late 1944 all of us were sent to clean bunkers on the Siegfried Line. The Germans expected the Americans to cross the Rhine here. Two meter-thick reinforced concrete bunkers were built directly on the bank of the river. They were equipped with circular windows for the defense, but stood empty. Over the years the inside of the bunkers got filled with leaves, branches, mud and spider webs. We took all the debris out and burned it. After the war I had the opportunity to watch how the French exploded these bunkers.

After we finished the clean-up, the *unter-officer* moved us further west near the city of Kaiserslautern in order to dig anti-tank trenches. We were supposed to dig alongside the locals, mainly young girls. The girls did not work much and mostly came to look at us. They would constantly bend over or crouch and 'unintentionally' expose themselves. Their behavior was difficult to describe without violating the rules of decency. American planes were flying over us in the clear skies. Perhaps to defend us from those wild girls, the pilots once fired at our construction site. Several people were taken out on stretchers.

After a few days we were ordered to move to another site. We went from the city of Kaiserslautern, meaning 'The Emperor's Lantern', to the hills of Kaiserstuhl, meaning 'The Emperor's seat'.

Both the city and the hills truly deserved their royal title. The hills were about the same height as the Vladimir hill in Kiev. From the top one could see the French border to the west and the Swiss Alps to the south. Ancient Romans had built the terraces and had grown grapes on the southwestern side. Very rational Germans had maintained these terraces in good condition over several centuries. The same rational Germans now decided to destroy the terraces and build anti-tank trenches.

As our favorite teacher Karl Marx once observed, "History repeats itself, first as tragedy, second as farce." Even Karl Marx could be right about one thing. I vividly remember how we dug anti-tank trenches in Kiev in 1941 and the tragedy which followed. Now we perceived our construction activities as pure comedy and behaved accordingly. Once we heard the sounds of the Allied aircraft above, we would immediately hide and sit deep in the trenches waiting until the end of the day. Even our commander, the old non-commissioned officer, understood the futility of our work, and often said:

"Ich habe die Schnauze full!" (I am fed up with this war!)

One day we saw several American planes flying very low to the West, and immediately after we saw over a horizon a thick black wall of smoke, following by huge fire. By my calculations, it was Weisweil.

Anticipation of freedom blinds a person to any other sensations. Feeling the imminent end of the war I lost any self-control. I went to my commander and asked to go to Weisweil and see if my Frau needed any help. The officer gave me a gloomy look and asked if I would rather go to the KZ (Concentration Camp), it was much closer and he could book my room there without a waiting list.

Incidentally, a couple of months after Liberation, as a free man, I decided to go and see what had happened in Weisweil. I did not know why. Probably I wanted to see Lena, the only bright memory I had during all of my stay in Germany. On Sunday I borrowed a bicycle from the farmer I was working for at the time, and within one hour I was in Weisweil.

I found nothing in the place where the village had once stood. It was flattened and the cute toy houses had turned into piles of ash. There was only one house still standing on the outskirts of the village. I went there expecting to see devastated people who had lost countless loved ones and all hard-earned possessions. I asked one lady if many people had died from the bombing. She joyfully smiled and said that no one was killed and that my former owners were living in one of the intact barracks.

I met Frau Anne and she told me that on the eve of the bombing an American aircraft flew very low and scattered leaflets with a warning that in retaliation for the barbaric bombing of a French village by the German aircraft, the village of Weisweil would be destroyed at 11 am the next day. In order to avoid unnecessary casualties all civilians were warned to leave the village in advance. At the exact time specified, the village was destroyed.

"Why are all these people so happy?" I inquired.

"Well, we all survived, which is cause for joy in and of itself. We managed to move all the cattle from the village to an open field. We saved all necessary tools. Most houses were insured. The war has ended. Life will only get better from here on out."

Unfortunately, Lena was nowhere to be found.

We talked about how humanely the Americans had waged this war. I could not help myself and told her about hundreds of burned houses in Russian villages and how the population had been deliberately pushed out to freeze in the winter.

I digress only to highlight common American behavior over the years, that is, whenever possible, avoid unnecessary casualties.

Now, back to the camp.

19. HOCHDORF

After finishing digging trenches, we were told that we were no longer needed in Weisweil, but there were other requests for our labor (the exact words of our guard were "there are other buyers").

The next morning a policeman arrived on a bicycle and took me, along with another prisoner, named Grisha, to the village of Hochdorf. There he handed us over to our new owners. The village was much smaller than Weisweil. One can tell the size of a village right away by the number of pubs on the main street: Weisweil had three while Hochdorf had none.

My new owner looked at me and asked where my belongings were. I showed him my pot and my spoon. He grinned and said, "Wash your hands and sit at the table."

This was something new. For the last three years no one had called me to sit at the table. He did not need to repeat the order. I quickly washed my hands in the sink located outside, like in Russian villages, and timidly entered the room not knowing what to do next.

"Sit down," he pointed to the table.

The entire family: his wife, his daughter-in-law and his grandson were already seated. I felt like a fish on a hot pan. I did not know how to behave and was afraid to make any mistakes. The owner noticed this and said, "Go and eat, otherwise you will not have enough strength to work."

This was the first decent meal I had had for a very long time. I remember it in detail. The wife poured me a plate of thick vegetable soup with no bread.

"Do you want more?" asked the owner.

"No, thanks," I said, trying not to push the limits.

The owner detected my hesitation and poured me another plate.

During the meal, I was asked countless questions - could I cut grass, could I milk cows, etc. After dinner the boss showed me my duties. At 6 am I was to get up and clean the cowshed with 8 cows and the stable with one horse, as tall as a skyscraper. Afterward I had to collect the manure into the concrete pit. Next I had to help the women with milking then cows. Then I could have my breakfast and go the fields to help the boss.

Among all the duties I agreed to do, I was only familiar with the one involving the horse. Even the horse was so huge that I could not imagine how to clean it. In any case I quickly realized that I had to work as hard as possible, so as to not be sent to another camp.

When I woke up at six that morning, the boss was already working in the fields. I cleaned the cowshed, the stable, and moved all the 'perfume' into the pit. The boss used the manure as a valuable fertilizer which we later took to the fields.

Around eight in the morning the wife and daughter-in-law came to milk the cows. I was afraid of milking and tried to stay in the stable as long as I could but it did not work. The owner ordered me to help the women, otherwise, he said, they would leave us without breakfast. I replied that cleaning the horse was so much fun that I could not stop.

Eventually I had to start milking. I knew that I should venture somewhere underneath the cow's udder and yank the cow's teats instead of her tail, but after a few minutes my cow started nervously backing up and slapping me with her tail. I asked Laura, the daughter-in-law, "What's up with this cow? Is she always nervous like that or just afraid of a stranger?"

"She is not nervous. You pull her teats so hard that she thinks you want to tear them off."

Laura showed me how to do it: gently squeeze the teats with the thumb and index fingers near the bottom and then use the rest of the fingers to further compress the teat.

At the end of the day I had finished only the 'half' of one cow by myself. The next day I had even better luck milking and I hoped that the cows and my boss were happy, the cows more so than my boss so that they would not keep whacking me with their tail. We put cans of milk outside of the gate near the road. I asked the boss if it was OK to leave the milk unguarded. He did not understand my question and responded that the milk car would arrive in the evening and carefully pick up the cans. The factory would measure the quantity of fat and at the end of the week send the boss a receipt and a check.

After breakfast, we harnessed the horse and went into the field. From that day on we worked in the fields from 9 am to 9 pm, except on Sundays. There was a small creek on the outskirts of the village. My boss had a personal area carved out by fences, where he was allowed to farm fish. Once he sent me to there to collect the fish harvest. Only bare-hand fishing was allowed. The fish were slippery but catching fish was much more pleasant than spreading manure. It was a rare case that I did better than my boss: I caught three fish while he caught only one.

My owner had many parcels of land in multiple locations around the village. From each piece of land he managed to squeeze out several harvests in one year. In one particular parcel we sowed beets and within one week we planted barley in the same location. I asked if these crops would affect each other. He explained that he would collect the barley harvest in June, while the beets would ripen by October.

I learned that his name was Fritz. In my opinion, he was a very intelligent farmer. Such successful and hard working farmers in Russia were called *kulaki*. They were arrested and sent to Siberia to feed the lice (at best) or the worms (at worst). In Germany such people fed the rest of the country.

In my perception, the family was very wealthy - eight cows, a horse, a lot of land - but their lifestyle was extremely modest, if not outright poor. In the several months I had worked for them I had never seen a piece of meat in their soup. They sold all their milk except for the one glass left for their child. I did not think this was fair and often helped myself to a sprinkle from a cow while milking her (it was hard to suppress my Soviet upbringing).

One day one of the women brought a piece of lard for a special occasion. The lard was completely covered with white worms. In more precise terms it was a large pile of worms with occasional pieces of lard visible on the surface. I thought I had tried everything in my life up to this point– dead horse meat, dirty potato skins, frozen potatoes - but this was the most disgusting food offered to me yet.

Fritz, observing my facial expression, said, "Don't be afraid of the worms you eat, be afraid of the worms that eat you."

The same worms most likely caused the riots on the Potemkin battleship, triggering the Russian revolution of 1905. I was not going to start riots. The lady boiled the lard, collected all the surfaced worms and divided the delicacy among everyone at the table. Following the family's example I quickly consumed my piece. Immediately I understood that the reason I had never tried spoiled lard during my captivity was because the guards would eat it first.

Besides those living in the house, the owner had two sons serving in the SS troops in Russia. There were no letters from them for a long time.

"They did not want to serve in the SS, but were forcibly conscripted," he added for some reason.

"Russia is not the best place to send a letter from," I tried to calm him down.

I offered him some spark of hope, but I clearly understood that after what the SS troops did in Russia, no Soviet soldier would deliver a captured SS-uniformed soldier to a camp alive.

The weather was nice and after work Fritz liked to sit outside on the porch and often invited me as company. He said that all the radios were confiscated after the Allies landed in France. He did not read newspapers but appraised the situation very realistically and did not fear saying that German defeat was inevitable. Perhaps, there was no Nazi party organization in the village and they did not know about the Gestapo. He spoke a lot about local affairs. In particular, he admitted that he did not love his wife and married her only because of a good dowry – a large piece of land. He mentioned it in the presence of his wife. I felt uncomfortable, but his wife did not visibly care.

Another time he told me that there was a large village nearby with a large Jewish population. It was very pleasant to conduct business with them. The Jews were reputable and honest people. The new regime took them somewhere, he did not know where. He knew that *halbes jüdisches* (half-Jews) were taken to concentration camps. German women liked to marry Jews because they were good providers and strong sexual partners.

On Sundays I did not work, which meant that I had to get up at 7 am, and only clean the stable and the cowshed, milk the cows and feed the cattle. The owner invited me to go to church, but I explained that I was Russian Orthodox and was not allowed to go to Catholic Church. This was the end of our theological discussions.

The villagers were not very social. I cannot remember a case of anyone visiting our family or our family going out. It was quiet all the time – even the dogs did not bark. The only diversity was supplied by a few people who were evacuated from the nearby city of Freiburg.

Freiburg was a small, picturesque university town located about two miles away, at the foot of the Schwarzwald mountain ridge. The town was divided by a small river. The east side was occupied by rich people living in cottages surrounded by lush gardens. Ordinary folks lived on the west side. One night Americans scattered leaflets warning about the upcoming bombing raid. Not everyone understood what the term bombing raid meant and only a few people left. The following night, the entire west part of the city was shaved off the face of the earth by the carpet bombing. There was not one bomb dropped on the eastern part. War had its own logic.

Incidentally, when in the 1990s my daughter was traveling in Europe, I asked her to bring some pictures from the sites where I had labored during the war. She brought some snapshots of the church, the main sight in the village. It was as small and pink as I remembered it. She also brought a photo of a small black granite slab with the names of soldiers killed during both world wars and the names of civilians who died during the Freiburg bombing.

I lived in a closet without windows and doors. My bed was a wooden box and my table was a smaller box. On sunny days I was able to read if the outside door was open.

There was a bookshelf in the kitchen and I was allowed to take some books to read. I found the main book of the German people – *Mein Kampf*, a few titles by Karl May, some history books and a few cheap fifteen-pfennig crime mysteries. I did not believe my eyes when I saw travel notes by Heinrich Heine *The Harz Journey*. I asked the owner whether he knew that he kept a banned book by a Jewish writer. He looked surprised:

"What are you talking about? I have no idea. Nobody reads books here. What did this Jew write?"

I showed him the book. He looked at the content and said, "I do not see anything illegal. It is a travel book about our region."

But the book was written by a Jew. Aren't you afraid that you could be punished for keeping it?"

"Who cares what books I keep at home? Maybe some of my boys brought it. They liked to read."

I began my studies with *Mein Kamp*". I could not find anything that I had not read already in all the newspapers. Only one chapter entitled "*Die Udenfrage*" (The Jewish Question) attracted my attention. Hitler wrote that he was sympathetic to this eternally torn nation with no home, which has to seek shelter in different countries. After that, he concluded that all the Jews, even the unborn ones, are potential Communists and carriers of the Bolshevik disease. The rest is well known.

I read another book, a history textbook with great interest. This book was published before Hitler's time and was not poisoned by fascist propaganda. There was objectivity in the assessment of historical events. As I read more and more, however, I came to the conclusion that there is no such thing as objective history; that history varies depending on who dictates the textbooks. I read for the first time that the Russian revolution was carried out by a small band of Bolsheviks, who were shipped in a sealed train car from Germany to Russia, that the revolution did not change anything – instead of a white czar the Communists set up the red czar. I was struck by the idea expressed in the book that after February of 1917 Russia had the opportunity to become a democratic nation of the European type, but missed this chance, prevented by a small group of conspirators led by Lenin.

I was brought up under Soviet propaganda and resented a lot of things written in this book. I felt particularly offended by its harsh portrayal of Lenin, who was considered a semi-God in the Soviet Union (from early childhood we learned that "Lenin lived, Lenin is alive, and Lenin will always be alive!")

But, on the other hand, I had also witnessed the terrible famine in Ukraine, which before the revolution was considered to be the 'Breadbasket of Europe'. I remember adults talking about confiscation of food and property, I remember the endless trials of traitors, spies and saboteurs who just a week before were 'Our Great Leaders'.

I cannot say that I turned my views around a full 180 degrees, but can definitely guarantee a ninety degree adjustment.

The last few months working for Fritz felt like an adventure to me. I worked extremely hard, sometimes dropping from exhaustion, especially after carrying packs of grass and barley. I often felt sharp pain in the bottom of my stomach, like I had felt in 1949 during my appendectomy without anesthesia. Fritz treated me well, not because I was a good worker, but because I tried to be a good worker. I was not afraid of being discovered as a Jew. I was out of the reach of the NKVD. I was not afraid of bombing. Every day the flying fortress few over us, but I saw them as messengers of my freedom.

One morning we saw a large German unit marching towards the forest. When we went to cut the grass we found a large pile of abandoned weapons - carbines, grenades, helmets, gas masks and other equipment. Near Fritz's parcel we found an enormous stack of artillery shells and mines, almost the size of the house. Among the abandoned weapons I found a small toy like handgun. It was so cute that I could not leave it behind. I promised Fritz to hide it away from the house - in the garden or near the church. He quietly observed the desertion and acknowledged the obvious, *"Alles ist kaput."*

20. FREEDOM

With little resistance, the Americans were moving forward very fast. My boss calculated that they would arrive at our village within a day or two. Villagers stayed indoors in anticipation of an invasion. The following day Fritz told me that the Americans were within three miles from the village and I was free to do whatever I wanted.

This happened on April 19, 1945.

I went to meet Grisha, who was working at the other end of the village. We decided to go to the city hall together and meet our liberators there. It is hard to describe our feelings at that time. The sun shone brightly on a completely empty village. Overwhelmed with anticipation and beaming with joy we waited. Suddenly, an open car filled with soldiers busted into the square. First they ordered us to put our hands up. When they saw our OST patches and recognized that we were Russians, they greeted us warmly, patted us on the backs and gave us some food and cigarettes.

It turned out that they were not American, but French. One of the soldiers was apparently Polish and, in that tongue, he facilitated our communication with the corporal in charge, using our broken Polish and his broken French.

The Pole asked me where I was from. "From Kiev," I replied. Then something unimaginable happened. He became red with rage, yelled something in Polish and with his rifle in hand he dragged me to the wall and cocked the rifle. I did not understand anything and froze. With great difficulty the corporal, assisted by his soldiers, pushed the Pole to the side and calmed him down. A little later we were told that after the German invasion, his village and his entire family had been slaughtered by Ukrainians from the neighboring village.

I tried to explain to the Pole that I had nothing to do with these atrocities and was captured during the first weeks of war. The Pole calmed down and described how he had escaped from Poland to Algeria, where he joined the French army.

After the war, I read memoirs by one partisan commander, in which he described in detail how the Poles slaughtered Ukrainian villages and how the Ukrainians slaughtered Polish villages before, during and immediately after World War II. This was a good illustration of the Soviet idea of 'Friendships of the Peoples'. Like in the old Soviet joke, a Jew has to pay with his life for the crimes committed by Ukrainian bandits against innocent Poles in retaliation for the crimes committed by Polish thugs against innocent Ukrainians.

This incident did not spoil the joy of meetings our allies, there was nothing that could break our spirit at that point. The corporal was appalled by our appearance and sent soldiers to the nearby hotel to bring us a change of clothing. He brought us to the hotel and ordered the owner to feed us until French administration was established in the village. The owners were trembling from fear and agreed to anything. Their two older sons had died in Russia, so we inherited their clothes. Next, the corporal went to a nearby two-story building housing Freiburg refugees and ordered them to assign us a room there.

Then the corporal looked at his watch and said that it was time for him to go. We asked him to take us, contending, "The war is not over yet, we want to join your unit and finish the common enemy." He said that he did not have the authority to do so, but promised to contact his superiors. We bid a warm farewell and the soldiers rushed ahead.

We faced the perennial question, "What now?" We felt like Russian peasants after the abolition of serfdom in Russia or like freed African slaves in America. We had our freedom, but what should we do with it?

Grisha decided to return to his former owner and wait until the situation was clarified. I could not decide on anything and went to settle in the room that had been assigned to us. The room was large and bright and had three beds. A fifteen-year-old boy was sitting at the table and nervously looking at me. He begged me for permission to remain living in this room, promising that he would not interfere.

The boy's name was Wilhelm and he had lost his parents during the Freiburg bombing. He had also been wounded in the bombing and had needed to stay in the hospital for an extended time, enduring multiple surgeries and surviving despite a negative prognosis. He showed me his stomach covered with terrible scars and stitches. He told me his story without much sorrow and with the abandon typical of a fifteen-year-old boy. I liked the boy and let him stay.

I was dizzy from emotional overload. My main thoughts were, "How would I get home, how would I prove my innocence?" I went to my former boss to say goodbye.

Fritz was much sober and reflective than I was. "Don't rush things," he said, "The war has not ended yet, the fighting continues. The end result is clear, but no one knows whether it will take weeks or months. Wait and look around. There is plenty of work in the field, and you can continue working for me. I will pay you for all the time since you began working here."

These were very reasonable words. I wanted to consider Fritz a very decent man, except for the fact that he was the father of two SS soldiers. We made a deal. I would continue living with Willie (the boy in my room) and work for Fritz every day starting at seven in the morning.

As the first order of business, Willie and I broke into the city hall through the window and took one of the confiscated radios (strictly on temporary basis, of course). The war was still going on, and I had a handgun. To my way of thinking, these facts made our actions fully justifiable wartime requisitions. We listened to the news the entire evening.

I began my workday at seven sharp and finished late at night. There was plenty of work. The most difficult task was cutting hay and barley. The easiest but most disgusting was collecting Colorado potato beetles. There were millions of them and they had voracious appetites for potatoes.

A most important change took place inside me. I did not have to think twice over each word I said. My boss treated me quite well. I took off the damned *OST* patch from my jacket (I still have this German souvenir) and I felt free. Fritz often sent me to Freiburg for errands. One day he gave me some money for a blacksmith and advised me to take the clothing I had to a tailor in Freiburg for a re-fit. On my way to the blacksmith I noticed that the butcher was selling meat for cash, without food vouchers. I stopped and bough about ten pounds of meat spending all the money I had. When I brought the meat home, Fritz and his wife were amazed and asked me to go back and buy more. Alas, it was too late: cash trade was prohibited the same day it began. Food vouchers were distributed and everything had disappeared once again.

I changed into civilian clothing and become a completely different person. To set myself apart from the Germans I inserted a red ribbon (the color of the Soviet flag) into my jacket's lapel. The Poles did the same with their colors. We wanted to show who the *herren* were and who the *narren* were now.

A few days later, Fritz sent me to Freiburg to sell several bags of barley. Meanwhile he went to the city hall and made me an ersatz document stating that *"Der Roman Kossowsky is als ein*

Landwirtschaftsarbeiter in der Gemeinde Hochdorf eingestelt," which meant that I was an agricultural worker in the village of Hochdorf. He also advised me to buy some pants in the store, because mine were too short. The shop owner demanded my purchase voucher for the pants. I said I didn't have one and showed him my POW document.

He refused to sell me anything. "I am not allowed to sell anything without a purchase voucher."

I began to demand my rights. "Don't you read the newspapers? Did the German soldiers present their vouchers when they robbed and killed people in my country? Do you need another bombing to realize that nobody needs Hitler and his vouchers?"

The vendor looked at me angrily but gave me a pair of trousers. He could not abandon his habits and nicely packed the trousers in a box with a nicely tied ribbon and thanked me for the purchase.

Every night I got my daily fix of joy from the radio. The Russians were fighting in Berlin; the Americans were rapidly moving east and the Germans were moving west even faster to surrender to the Americans. One day Fritz told me in pigeon German the most important news himself, "Hitler made *kaput*." It was not clear how Hitler had done it – by shooting or poisoning himself - but it did not matter, he was dead. The Germans capitulated in a few days.

However, I heard not only the good news but along with the rest of the world I learned about the atrocities committed in concentration camps and about the gas chambers. Newspapers published the first images from newly liberated camps of stacks of corpses near gas chambers.

There were rumors about looting in Freiburg. Fritz told me that most of the looting had been done by the Russians living in the nearby camp for displaced persons. Some got a hold of weapons and at night raided wealthy homes. He complained that often the victims were innocent people, while the hardened Nazis remained unpunished. He even named several names and addresses. I was not sure why he mentioned these names and addresses; I mean, was it his sincere indignation toward the Nazis or because of a desire to settle some personal scores? In either event, I did not react.

Willie and I became good roommates. He found an old phonograph with a few disks, including some soundtracks from Charlie Chaplin's films. Gradually our room morphed into the local dance spot. The village girls were rather shy and initially just stopped by to listen to the music, but soon they become more relaxed and assertive. There were very few young men left in the village, and the girls liked to dance. Willie spent all his spare time fixing the rifle he found and I had to assume the full burden of dance responsibilities. As it happened, the local dance etiquette required the partners to press as close as possible to each other. I followed these rules quite well.

One evening Fritz joked at dinner, "Listen, Roman, there are rumors that you 'tried' every girl in the village and now they are all damaged goods!"

"Did anyone complain?" I replied. "If they do, put these damaged goods on my tab as part of the German reparations."

Fritz laughed. His daughter-in-law Laura laughed even harder and also blushed.

I really liked some of the girls. One had been evacuated from Freiburg and she sometimes asked me to walk her home to a small house that she shared with her grandmother. The house was set in the forest high in the mountains. I knew the walk would be long and happily obliged.

The dancing did not stop my endless worrying about my future. I wanted to go home even more than before, but I heard reports that all Russian POWs and displaced persons who had been fortunate enough to survive were being sent to Siberia. Most POWs were convicted of treason and sent to the camps for ten years of hard labor. The British in their zone of occupation were forcibly transferring all displaced Russians to the custody of the Soviet authorities. The Americans sent only those willing to go home. Freiburg was in the French zone and was full of posters inviting former prisoners to work in France or sign up for the French Foreign Legion.

I started noticing changes in Laura's behavior. Anything I said would cause her to giggle, blush and behave strangely. Perhaps she was tired of constantly waiting for her husband to come back and I was right there, available and dancing with other girls. Fritz also noticed it and in early July he started the following conversation with me:

166

"Recently, I noticed that you walk as if your thoughts are elsewhere. You are sick and your disease is called *heimsucht* (home sickness). I don't think it makes sense for you to wait until they start the rail service or provide other forms of transportation to get where you want to go. You are an urban guy and will not be happy living in the village. I can help you. I can give you my bike, the money that you earned, and a little food and this way you will reach the Soviet occupation zone in about a week. Think about it and let me know."

I liked his idea. I could not wait until the next morning to tell Fritz that I agreed. We fixed the bicycle, and packed a loaf of bread and some cheese. Fritz gave me the money and two bottles of moonshine (It occurred to me that I had never seen him moonshining). He said that moonshine was more valuable than money. He gave me a map and advised me on how to behave on the road.

The farewell was short and I started my personal *'Drang Nach Osten'*. I was happy; whatever would be would be. The road was empty, like it was built for me alone. The bike smoothly rolled forward. I left behind war, danger, death. I was looking forward to meeting new people and starting my new life.

My first encounter did not take too long. I saw the blond girl I used to walk to her grandma's. I thought there would be a touching, romantic goodbye, but I was mistaken. The girl just gave me a sealed letter and asked me to pass it to her fiancée who fought somewhere on the Eastern front and was probably captured. To her understanding, Russia and Ukraine were akin to Freiburg and Hochdorf and it was simply impossible to miss her boyfriend there. At first I promised to do what I could, but then I imagined myself crossing into the Soviet zone and being searched by the NKVD while carrying a sealed letter written in German. There would be no way that I would not be shot on the spot as a spy. I could not explain all this to the girl, so I just asked how her grandma was and said goodbye.

Every two-three miles I passed another village. They were all picturesque and beautiful and even the dreadful stink of manure from adjacent fields could not spoil my idyllic mood. After a while I found a wider and busier road. A large column of American cars passed me so closely that I almost got sucked under their wheels. I turned my face toward the column so the drivers could see my red ribbon and frantically waved my arms, but the drivers did not see me. By noon I had reached Baden-Baden. I remembered that this was the place where Dostoevsky had written his best works and had gambled away all his hard-earned money; where Turgenev had worked on his most insightful novels about Russian life and where Gogol either wrote or burned his defining work *Dead Souls*. There was a banner near the fork in the road which said "Keep silent, people are resting." I thought about it a little and took the road bypassing this gambling oasis.

Not having a watch, I kept time by the sun. When I realize that the day came to an end I become tired and craved rest. It was hot and I wore a heavy wool jacket that I was afraid to take off, since I did not have anything decent underneath and needed to look presentable in order to find a place to sleep. I was drunk off of my new freedom and did not realize that I had already traveled about fifty miles. After a short rest under a tree I tried to go further, but my feet did not want to follow.

In the next village I asked for a place to sleep. The owner offered me a pile of hay. I ate what Fritz gave me and fell asleep. I slept for about ten hours and woke up to loud talking. I opened my eyes and found a young girl next to me.

"How did you get here?" I asked surprised.

"I asked for a place to sleep. The owner sent me here. It was late, very dark and I did not realize that I was not alone in this 'apartment'," she answered.

She was German, just freed from a concentration camp. She avoided my questions on how she got there and I lost any interest in her. The owner offered us a modest breakfast and we went on our separate ways.

There were long and winding roads, scenic places, small villages, neat houses. My legs were tired and I could not push the pedals as fast as they did in the onset of my journey. I stopped in one town for a beer. It was one of those ersatz tasteless beers, but still cold and refreshing. As I left the pub I noticed a poster that looked strangely familiar. Against the backdrop of blue sky and golden wheat fields an old man and woman, gray and drawn, were looking at the horizon, holding hands, the woman wiping tears from her eyes. The text in Russian said, "Son, where are you?" and below, "The Motherland awaits you." I knew that it was the usual brute Soviet propaganda, but the inscription somewhat touched me. Perhaps I yearned for my motherland to wait for me. This is why the posters were invented - to inspire hope. The poster looked so moving that I wanted to believe it. I sincerely hoped that after the bloody carnage I had witnessed, things would change for the better.

A group of American officers stopped for a beer. These were the first Americans I had met on the road. Suddenly, I noticed a Russian officer among them. I also noticed that he was wearing golden epaulets, like the Czarist Russian army uniform (at that time I did not know that the Soviet Army had adopted czarist – the uniform style around 1943 or 1944). I could imagine what was waiting for this young and handsome officer after he would return home - he was in the American occupation zone, in contact with Americans, therefore a typical spy.

After the previous day's marathon, I decided to moderate my speed and stop more often. As soon as I reached a large village, as Fritz advised me, I went to the Mayor to ask for a place to sleep.

Like every person, every village has a face defined by a meld of houses, terrain, the central square, the church on the square, and assorted 'cultural establishments' (pubs) punctuating the village surrounds. Some villages have houses surrounded by lush greenery; others bring farms and barns to the forefront. This was particularly true in Germany, which had been unified only recently (during the Bismarck's time in the late 19th century). In some villages, located only two or three miles from each other, people spoke unintelligible languages and dialects; some were so different that they did not even sound German. The villagers had to use *Hoch Deutsch*, a literary state language to communicate with outsiders.

The face of this particular village was defined by the Mayor's house. It was the largest and architecturally the most unique house in the village.

Someone met me at the door. I was not sure whether he was a butler or a servant. He asked about the purpose of my visit and led me through the long corridor to a large reception room. He told me that he would announce me to Herr von Kronberg. The corridor and reception were adorned with large portraits, depicting the ancestors of the Herr. Some portraits were of men in medieval armor, others showed various hunting scenes. I was awed and intimidated from such grandeur and immediately regretted coming here. I waited for a long time. Finally the Mayor showed up.

He was not very friendly and after listening to me angrily asked, "Is this why you bother me?"

"Yes, Sir," I talked back to him, "I got bored in the concentration camp and decided to go home!"

I recount this episode now purely for bragging rights. I met a real 'Von'. I can relate to an old anecdote by Shalom Aleichem about a Jew who liked to brag in his schtetl that he had met and had spoken with the governor.

"And what did you talk about?" the villagers asked.

"Nothing special. He was passing by and I said, 'How do you do, Your Excellency!' and he replied, 'Go to Hell, stinking Jew!'"

The Mayor's servant sent me to a rundown house with no traces of useful furniture. Such houses were typical for Russia but quite rare for Germany.

The owner of the house was a skinny and withered person of about fifty-five years old. He was very excited after finding out that I was Russian. He told me how much he loves the Soviet Union and that Communism is the only decent form of the human society. I interrupted him and asked if he had some hot tea or coffee. Embarrassed, he said that he had just run out of all provisions, but after he would get his money tomorrow, he would definitely treat me to real German *knudels*. I was not going to wait around for *knudels* and pulled out my own bread and cheese. Judging by the owner's stare, I realized that unless I shared my meal with him I would not be able to continue in peace and tranquility. After finishing my bread, the owner became even friendlier and tried to persuade me not to go to Russia and instead stay with him. I asked how he was planning to support himself. He owned neither land nor the smallest garden; his house was barely standing, he did not even have a kettle to boil water. He ignored all my questions.

I could not imagine how it was possible that in a village always in need of a pair of working hands, one could not earn enough for a piece of bread. I realized that I had met a true German *schlimazel*. In the morning, I arose early and left before breakfast.

After a while, I stopped for some food and beer in a small town. The owner brought me the beer but requested a voucher for food. I told him that I was returning home from captivity and he brought me food for free. We started a conversation. The owner told me about a train to Schweinfurt, which was being formed at the nearby railway station. There was a big Russian camp near the town of Schweinfurt. I checked the map. This town was somewhat away from my route, but I became interested. In fact, the train was about to depart from the station at any minute. It was a freight train, so nobody asked for tickets. I took a seat on an open platform car, next to several women and children.

During this trip I 'used' my handgun for the first time. When I had found this gun, it was empty. Willie liked my small gun very much and did not stop until he found some visibly suitable cartridges. We tried to fire them but only one out of six attempts resulted in actually firing of a bullet, which flew for about two yards. Willie begged me to leave him the gun, but I loved it and took it with me. Again, I resembled a character from a Shalom Aleichem story.

"The hero was wearing glasses; one eye was without a lens, another one covered by a thin paper. When asked why he wears them, he answered 'Es iz fort a briln' (these are still glasses)."

Right after the train had taken off; a tall and heavy man about forty years old jumped on the car platform and took a seat next to a woman. They were talking about something and I was daydreaming next to my bicycle on the other edge of the platform.

The sun shone brightly, the train moved slowly and the road read boring. Suddenly this fellow saw my red ribbon. His face beaming with anger, he stood up and approached me, screaming, "Look, these people are to blame for our losing the war, we need to do something, we cannot sit here next to them!" The women were scared but did not say anything. The distance between us was getting shorter and shorter and when it became about four yards I pulled out my revolver and spun the cylinder to make it clear that it was loaded. At the first sight of the gun the fellow quickly returned to his seat as if nothing had happened.

But I became so pumped up, that I could not restrain myself and started screaming at him, "*Du-verfluchter schweinehund*", I taunted, "you spilled blood all over Europe, you wanted to destroy my people and turned them into slaves. It is because of you that all of Germany is now in ruins and millions of families have lost their breadwinners. Do you remember screaming *Heute gehert uns Deutschland und morgen die ganze Welt* (Germany belongs to us today, but tomorrow the whole world will be ours) during your sick Nazi rallies? If you had a slightest drop of conscience you would kill yourself as your beloved Fuhrer did!"

I did not know if he had understood my tirade, but after seeing my gun and my angry face he decided to hide in the corner behind the women. At the next station I looked for American MPs to arrest this Nazi, but he doubtless had jumped off the train even before we arrived at the station.

174

The station and the town of Schweinfurt looked miserable. The town was bombed into ruins because it had had a lot of military targets. A new road had been cleared through the middle of the ruins, leading directly to the camp, which consisted of two large barracks.

I asked people loitering around the camp, "Who are you? What kind of camp is this?"

"We are Russian POWs. And what kind of camp to you need?" they rejoined with caution.

I told them my story. They listened carefully, but did not ask any questions. Since they seemed incapable of providing any sensible answers I made my way to the office where the authorities were.

In the reception I met the camp administrator who wore a white band on his sleeve. There was a large portrait of Czar Nicholas II hanging on the wall surrounded by a number of church icons. A church service was being held next door. The administrator was a very friendly man, obviously from the czarist times. He used the pre-revolutionary words like 'Sir', 'Mister', 'Would you please?' which sounded foreign to me. I grew up calling people 'comrades'. I told him that I was not sure about my future plan, I wanted to go home, but was afraid of the NKVD. I asked to spend the night and he saw to it that I got a place in a hostel and two vouchers for dinner and breakfast.

There were several people in the dining room but I found it difficult to become acquainted with them. From random pieces of conversations that I overheard I realized that this was not *my* camp. It was run by Monarchists and *quislings* – those who had been cooperating with Nazis. After spending one night I hit the road again.

I became so accustomed to the awe-inspiring scenery of south-western Germany that the road east from Schweinfurt looked to me like God's punishment. It ran through a monotonous semi-arid plain with no trees, no villages and no places to rest. Only rarely a car would pass, often burning me with the heat of its engine.

Within a few hours the road went downhill and after a turn an unbelievable bird's eye view of a vast green valley opened up below, with multi-colored boxes of fields and gardens, green and red tiled pointed roofs and the characteristic high church spires. It offered such a stark contrast with the semi-desert I had ridden through before, that I had to stop for a few minutes and sit under a tree to admire the scenery.

The road continued sharply downhill and brought me to a house where an old man was working in the front garden. I stopped and asked for water. He called someone inside, and an old woman emerged holding a jug of water. She asked if I wanted to wash my hands. I said yes and she brought me a towel. I was shocked – it was a typical Ukrainian *rushnyk* – a traditional towel embroidered with roosters and crosses.

Just in case, I asked, "Has someone brought this towel from Ukraine or did you embroider it yourself?"

The woman said that it was Tanya who had embroidered the towel and told me her story. She and her husband were an elderly childless couple in failing health and unable to manage their farm. Three years earlier they had received an *Ostarbeiter* from Russia. They fell in love with this great girl and wanted to adopt her, but the authorities refused to permit it. Now with the war ended, they wanted to adopt her again and devise all their possessions to her. Complicating the situation, Tanya could not decide whether she wanted to stay or to return home. They could not imagine their life without Tanya, the old lady said with tears in her eyes.

Tanya was a typical Ukrainian girl, lean and beautiful, about twenty years old. We spoke Ukrainian. In 1942 all the youth from her village in the Chernigov region were taken to Germany. In the beginning she received several letters from her mother, but then all mail stopped. She found out that her native village was burned down, but she did not know whether her mother was still alive. Life in Germany was very difficult for her - she missed her home, her language, her family. The owners were very nice, but she felt like a stranger and had not made any friends. Picking a moment when Tanya was looking away, the old lady asked me if I could persuade the girl to stay.

While we were talking the sun began to go down. The owners offered for me to stay and I was happy to sleep in a haystack. In the morning Tanya asked for my advice. I told her that I was on my way home, but had not yet decided if it was the right choice. After hearing all these terrible stories coming from Russia, I was unable to make a final decision.

I advised her, "Do not rush. No one is kicking you out. Unlike me, you have a roof over your head. Try to find out if any of your family survived in your village. Any decision you make now you can just as easily make a year from now."

Tanya took a deep breath, but did not answer. I understood how difficult this decision would be for her.

In the morning the owners pointed me in the direction of the Soviet occupation zone. I had to drive 800 yards, join the highway and drive through the spa town of Bad Stolberg. The total distance was about thirty miles. This town hosted the headquarters of a large American army command and no strangers were allowed in.

In about two hours, I had reached the first American checkpoint. The checkpoint consisted of a tent, a small gate across the road and a soldier sitting under a nearby tree reading a book. I stopped and greeted the soldier. He reluctantly put his book away, and asked in passable German for *Papieren* (Documents). He barely glanced at the paper which my former owner had given me and waved me through. I tried to turn my left side toward him so he could see my red ribbon, but he did not care and did not even say, "*Auf Wiedersehen.*"

My next meeting with the Americans happened in a few hours. The second checkpoint was much more substantial – the road was blocked by an armored personnel carrier. The soldiers saw my red ribbon and recognized an ally. They put me along with my bicycle into the truck and drove me to the army headquarters in the city of Mulheim. The border between the Soviet and American zones of occupations was about seven miles away.

The commander issued me a real document certifying that I was indeed who I claimed to be. I signed the document with my thumbprint and became a legitimate person once again. At the end of the procedure, I asked if they might point me to a place to sleep. Ben, the American who spoke German, gave me the address of the apartment where he lived and told me that I could share a room with a boy named Kurt.

The boy was about fourteen years old. I told him that Ben had sent me and he let me in. His family owned the house and Ben was his mother's boyfriend. His father had disappeared somewhere in Russia. Kurt was in complete awe of the American. Ben let the boy play with his handgun. He also shared his nude magazines with him, which must have had sealed the deal. We quickly found a common language. I showed him my small revolver and promised to give it to him should I go to the Soviet zone. I knew I had to give up the gun before crossing to the Soviet zone. This bought me a 'lifelong' friend. As a sign of eternal friendship Kurt gave me a chocolate bar, part of Ben's supplies. The last time I had seen chocolate was several years ago in a large showcase store in Kiev. Kurt's mother came home by the end of the day. She was a rather fat woman, about fifty years old. After Kurt said that Ben had sent me, she prepared a meal for us.

The next day was the most difficult for me since I had been liberated by the French soldiers. After breakfast I headed to the border. I was in a strange state of mind, like a person preparing to jump from a cliff into a body of water without knowing if he could swim. My mind told me to stop and do not push my luck. My heart yearned to go home. My mind and heart did not get along, but ultimately my heart won out.

There were two gates across the road – one American and one Russian. The American soldier looked at my papers and raised the gate without any questions. Next was the Russian soldier. I told him that I wanted to return home from captivity. He refused to let me in and told me that I could return only in an organized way through existing camp procedures. I did not know whether to regret or rejoice this postponement. I waited for a while and then decided to go back. For a moment I was afraid that the American would not let me back, but he immediately raised the gate.

I went to search for a proper camp. This was not easy. The camps were located in big cities, but I had to use rural roads where it was easier to find a place to sleep. Sometimes the owners offered me meals, and other times I had to work for food.

I remember a particularly curious incident. I agreed to clean a henhouse in exchange for dinner and breakfast. My mistake was that I agreed to do so before seeing the henhouse first. When I finally saw it, I realized that Hercules had it very easy with his Augean stables compared to this shack full of chicken shit.

I was hungry and had no choice but to start working. Once I bent over to pick up another pile of manure I suddenly felt a sharp bite on my head. I turned around to see a huge rooster in full fighting mode, sitting on a plank and screaming loudly, challenging me to a fight. And a fight he got. He had an advantage – like a fighter aircraft he could fly around. My weapon was only a rake. Our chances were about equal. The fight ended by my clobbering the bird with my rake and forcing him into the corner of the loft. The rooster proudly screamed from there, probably bragging to the hens about his success. He did manage to bite me several times and had bloodied me, but I still think I won the exchange.

I showed the owner my scratches and received an extra three-egg omelet as reparations.

"It is strange - the rooster usually behaves well," the owner said.

"Yes, and that is why you have such a huge pile of shit in a barn," I replied.

I decided to concentrate my movement along big cities where I figured I had better chances of finding camps with former prisoners of war. Stuttgart was the closest big city on my way and I decided to go there. Within seven miles of the city I got caught in a strong storm. In a few seconds I was completely soaked. It was dangerous to cycle on a wet road dodging heavy traffic and it was even more dangerous to drive on the shoulder because of the slippery cliffs.

Eventually, my bicycle wheel started resembling the number '8' and it was impossible to ride any more. I had to hand-carry the bicycle to the nearest village, where the Mayor sent me to a priest's house to spend the night.

The priest lived in a big, beautiful house in the center of the village, in front of the church. The priest was very friendly and introduced himself as Father Jurgen. He lived with his sister's family. He asked me where I would prefer to sleep - in the barn or inside. I chose the barn. The priest invited me inside and asked his sister to bring me dinner. The sister smiled strangely the entire time.

The priest stayed during dinner and paid ever increasing attention to me. After the usual questions of, "who, where and how", he told me that he had just recently returned from a concentration camp, and was very sympathetic to my situation. After dinner he brought me a large piece of cake and asked whether I had dry clothes and if I needed money. He invited me to the following day's service in his church, noting that the parishioners were very fond of listening to his sermons. I thanked him and politely refused, saying that Russian Orthodox Christians are not allowed to pray in Catholic churches.

Sunday was a real day off for me. I lay on the haystack, reading newspapers and magazines that I had found in the house. From my vantage point I could observe the square in front of the church. A seemingly unending flow of people headed to church to listen to the sermon.

In the afternoon the priest came to the barn and asked if I was bored. He suggested going to the nearby village, to the workshop where they could fix my bicycle. He offered to show me the way there. Then he started telling me about all the problems I would face if I returned to the Soviet Union. He suggested that I go to Stuttgart and find a job in the U.S. military administration. Then he began to tell me about himself. He owned a castle in the Alps and offered for me an opportunity to work there for him as a driver. He promised to treat me well. He would not have objections if I decided to marry someday. He already had a Russian 'friend' in the camp, whom he had helped with various provisions and cigarettes. He went on to explain that he was quite rich and would not mind giving me enough money to meet my needs.

Slowly I put two and two together and understood the strange smiles of his sister, his very unusual attention to me and the reason he ended up in a concentration camp. Nazis did not like either Catholic priests or gays very much.

I was thinking about spitting in his face, but he had been very polite and tactful and I decided to continue and to not blow him off. I pretended not to understand his hints. After a while, I got fed up with these games and told him that I understood his proposal, thanked him for his concern, but could not accept his offer.

I also added, "My religion does not allow such things and I wonder how a man of faith, like you, can propose this to me?"

He was not very embarrassed by my reference to religion, "I have not suggested anything bad, why don't you think about my proposal?"

On Monday after prayers in church, as if nothing had happened, he reminded me that we should go to a neighboring village to fix my bicycle's wheel. I had already taken the wheel off in anticipation.

"Do you mind if I go with you and show you the way?" he asked.

"Certainly. You can help me carry the wheel," I joked.

The narrow trail passed through scenic areas. The priest was walking behind me and kept talking the whole time, mostly about political and religious topics. He admitted that he was a great sinner, but hoped that God would forgive him if he prayed hard. I did not participate in the conversation and my thoughts were elsewhere. When crossing a small stream the priest asked if he could hold my hand to help his balance. He grasped my hand, quite easily jumped over the stream and suddenly kissed me on the cheek. Surprised, I pushed him away strongly and he fell into the stream. Watching him getting out was very funny and I laughed.

"Why are you laughing?" he protested with palpable resentment, "I have had much more beautiful boys than you!"

I continued laughing and said that I could find the shop by myself.

"Ok, I will go with you, just let me dry out a little."

I suppose that for him physical attraction was stronger than his resentment. The incident had not perturbed him even a bit and he insisted that he pay the blacksmith for his work. I allowed him this pleasure.

I really liked Jurgen's idea of applying for work in the American administration and waiting out the uncertain times. I thought if I worked for a year among the Americans, I would learn English and would be able to speak two foreign languages. This could be a profession in itself when I returned home. I was already twenty-one years old and the only professional abilities I had were milking cows and cleaning up manure. Not much.

I went to Stuttgart. I quickly found the administration building and was sent to a colonel. He was sitting in an enormous room next to a huge vicious looking German shepherd. The colonel was very friendly. He carefully listened to me but did not understand a word. His assistant translated in one of the Slavic languages and eventually I understood that the colonel had been assigned to this position only a day before and did not know for sure what to do. He asked me to come back in a week when he would be able to help me.

Again, I was facing a painful unknown. I really liked the colonel. He genuinely tried to understand me, spent a lot of time discussing my case with his assistant and I was sure he would help me out with a job. But at the same time, how would I eventually explain to the NKVD that I had worked for Americans for some time instead of rushing back to my Motherland? I realized that by seeking employment in the American zone, I was just delaying the inevitable – my return to the place where I truly belonged. I finally made up my mind.

I learned that in about forty miles from Stuttgart there was a camp for displaced persons. In three days I arrived there. The camp was located in the former monastery building. The building looked like a sixteenth century castle – massive walls, narrow windows, forged doors. I felt a pervasive and invisible influence of knights, armored horses and other medieval exotica. The door from the reception room led to the monastery proper. This was a remarkable door, almost a gate, with steel rivets, inspection windows and other architectural excesses, probably intended to emphasize the solemnest of this edifice.

The left door led to a more modern building. It was a large barrack-style room divided in sections by low wooden partitions. During the war this room housed a German military hospital, run by monastery nuns. Americans had now allocated this empty room for displaced persons who wanted to return to Russia. The monastery continued to run the daily affairs of the camp, as they had done for the hospital. On the day of my arrival the population of the camp was about thirty people, including about twenty women. It increased every day by three or four people. The camp manager was an elderly woman who like most people here, was brought to Germany as a forced laborer. She put our names on the list and passed it to a nun. The nun brought us some food.

The food reminded me of the worst days of my life in the POW camp. The portion was not enough for a small child, let alone for a normal healthy adult. On the second or third day we were ready for a riot. The three of us with the best knowledge of the German language were selected to serve as negotiators. We knocked on the locked iron doors of the monastery. A scared nun opened the window and asked what we needed.

"We must speak with the sister responsible for our food. We are starving."

"She is busy praying."

"Please let us in, we will wait inside."

"No, entry to outsiders is forbidden."

"OK. We will wait outside, but we cannot do it for a long time – we are starving."

"Well, I will report this matter to the senior sister."

We waited for a long time. People started losing patience, but I felt that we must maintain our calm and adhere to appropriate etiquette. It was still a monastery in the territory occupied by the Allies. It was not clear how they would react if we started a scandal. Finally, the senior num arrived.

"We are starving. Now, honestly, where did you find the menu you feed us from - Buchenwald or Auschwitz?"

"We have difficulties with the product voucher system. We fed the same meals to wounded soldiers."

"That's why they lost the war."

At this moment one of the delegates, a quite elderly man, rudely interrupted this diplomacy using one word: *Schweinerai* (Disgusting mess). Maybe this was the only German word he knew, but the result was startling.

The sister forgot that outsiders could not enter the monastery, opened the door and asked us to come in and wait while she reported this matter to an even more superior sister. This time, the wait was very short.

A very proper looking nun came down and through her stiff lips asked, "What is the matter?"

"We already explained our complaints to the others. They were supposed to report the nature of our complaints. For four years we worked in German captivity and were permanently hungry. Now we deserve decent food. During our stay in your camp we never saw a piece of meat. We are starving. If you do not provide us with enough food, we will ask the American Administration for help."

The nun gave us a dismissive look and through her tightly pursed lips promised to follow up and left. The same day our food improved dramatically.

To call our place a camp would be a misuse of this word and an insult to the Americans. We enjoyed absolute freedom. There was a guard near the entrance, but we could come and go as we pleased. I think that the guard was supposed to protect the women, who were the majority here, from possible attacks by the local population. However, his main responsibility seemed to be to flash a smile when we passed by. He did a great job.

One day the American officers decided to set up a reception in honor of our women. Our women were poorly equipped to participate in an international ball, but their ingenuity in making makeshift outfits saved the day. We stood by the window, listening to the music and someone even climbed a tree to see our women dancing inside with GIs. Contrary to our expectations, the ball had ended quite early and we received a full report: they served only non-alcoholic beverages and small but very tasty sandwiches. The bread was very white and puffy, but tasted like cotton. The officers were polite and gallant, and the women thoroughly enjoyed the event. We also were happy – the absence of vodka offset our resentment of the fact that men were not invited.

While walking in the city, we found a great, almost Olympic size swimming pool. There was a sign on the entrance: "Only for American soldiers." Using hand gestures we timidly asked the guard if we, Russian prisoners of war, could enjoy a swim. He said "OK." From that moment my friend and I spent all out time in the pool, barely emerging from the water. We felt wonderful. Could we ever imagine a situation when the Germans were barred from their own pool, but we, 'the inferior race', were allowed? They used to thing *"Deutschland, Deutschland uber alles!"* and now they got what they deserved! The weather was splendid. Undressed, we did not look much different from the Americans, and sometimes the soldiers mistook us for their own and tried to talk to us.

Another soldier decided that we were Germans and began to speak to us in Yiddish, thinking that he was speaking German. I answered in German thinking that I was speaking in Yiddish (which I had thoroughly forgotten). He was from Brooklyn and had been in combat for two years. He showed us some photographs and offered us cigarettes.

Another time two Germans were waiting for us at the exit of the pool. They carefully looked around, as if planning something forbidden. One of them asked:

"Are you Russians?"

"Yes," I replied.

"Do you speak German?"

"A little."

"We are Communists. While Hitler was in power, we went underground. Now we are looking to connect with our Russian comrades. Do you have any orders for us?"

At first, I thought they were crazy. No normal person would ask such a question to a stranger.

"What kind of orders do you have in mind?" I asked.

It suddenly occurred to me that they may be harboring some crazy ideas, like blowing up some building deemed capitalistic. They whispered among themselves for a while and told us that they would come back tomorrow. Fortunately, we never saw them again, but often laughed remembering these *kameraden*.

I often return to this episode, and attempt to fathom what compels people to be so loyal to an idea, even if the idea is clearly

190

wrong or evil. Indeed, a few of such ideas throughout history have been adopted and promoted by a very small group of people, and have led to the enslavement of millions. When I looked at the peaceful Germans I could not believe that these were the same 'good Germans' who had screamed "Zig Heil" [24] *to the raving ideas of their crazy Fuhrer. They behaved as if they had just woken up after a hypnotic sleep, opened their eyes and could not believe what they had done. The most enlightened and prosperous country in Europe had become a pathetic shadow of its former greatness.*

The same happened to Russia. A great country with great intellectual potential and vast resources had been on its way to becoming a modern democratic society. A handful of conspirators infected the country with the ideas of communism, blinded the population with false slogans and as a result the majestic double-headed eagle gradually turned into a defeathered chicken.

Everything good must come to an end. I often doubted this day would ever come, but finally two big trucks arrived and moved us to another sprawling camp. There were no doubts left that this was a CAMP, and not something else. Two large men with red armbands met us in front of two huge iron gates. It was obvious that they were not former prisoners of war; their gross shouts accurately pointed to what organization they belonged.

---

[24] *Sieg Heil!* - a common Nazi salute recited by the party faithful. Literally, it means Hail (to) Victory.

21. RUSSIA STARTS IN GERMANY

An American soldier guarding the gate was just for show. The people with armbands controlled everything in the camp. All empty surfaces were taken up by portraits of Stalin and various Soviet slogans. Despite a varied assortment of posters, every one of them referred in some way to 'Our Great Leader'. We realized that we had indeed arrived home. I recalled the words of Pushkin, "*Here is our Russian spirit, here is our Russian smell.*" During my time away, I thoroughly forgot about this overwhelming propaganda, but I was acutely aware that this was my new life and I had to adapt to it.

The only way out of the camp was through the gates. Every time when I accidently approached the gate, people with armbands firmly told me that it was prohibited to come close to the entrance. I realized that this gate fulfilled only one role – that of entrance, but not of exit.

To enrich our political consciousness we were forced to attend daily lectures from which we learned everything we needed to know about the glorious Communist Party, its Great Leader and the Superior Communist Theory, which was 'True because it is correct' or 'Correct because it is true', or something like this.

The slogans also mentioned "The Great Victory over Germany", but the same slogans were absolutely clear that we the victory was to be attributed to Generalissimo Comrade Stalin, and then to the Russian people, in that order. The camp looked like a Soviet camp was supposed to look: gray, unwelcoming, depressing, a dead end. People roamed idly in the yard, played cards or slept in hot cells.

Once, loitering in the yard, I heard music from the corner where the superiors lived. A warm voice chanted wartime songs, like "Wait for Me", "Dark Night", "Raise Up, the Vast Country." I could not move away from that location until the music ended. My eyes become wet and I got goosebumps on my skin when I listened to "Rise Up, the Vast Country." Those were the famous war songs which until this day are a part of Russian culture, but I was hearing them for the first time. I realized why I wanted to go home so badly. Russia was not just the NKVD, there were people in Russia who sincerely loved their country and wrote and sang such beautiful songs.

After one week in the camp, after our superiors decided that we had had enough training to fully realize the greatness of Stalin, we were loaded onto a freight train and taken to the Soviet occupation zone of Germany. When crossing the demarcation line I did not see a single soldier guarding the American side. At the same time on the Soviet side, as far as eyes could see, a Soviet soldier was posted in intervals of 100-150 yards. They were guarding 'The Freest Country in the World'.

The train stopped at the station and we were ordered to get out and form two lines. After the American train returned to the

West, two armed guards were assigned to each line. We got the hint. The previously happy and chatty crowd eagerly anticipating their homecoming became q gloomy and developed the quiet disposition of prisoner. The sweet smoke of the Motherland was getting sootier and sootier.

We were ordered to surrender our knives, cameras, bicycles, maps, radios, watches, and other such personal items. I anticipated that we would not be allowed to bring such luxury items into the country and in advance had traded my bike for a pair of good shoes. I dumped the map of Germany given to me by Fritz into the pile of garbage. The word 'map' in this situation would be associated only with the word 'espionage'.

We continued to wait and wait and wait. Two officers came by and asked for several people with high school education. Four of us were picked and taken off the train to assist with the local army administration. The Lieutenant, who was quite friendly, explained that we had to register Italian POWs on their way home to Italy from Soviet camps. We were put in a dormitory and received our food from the officer's cafeteria. We felt very comfortable. We were supposed to fill out a registration card for every Italian to be transferred to the American occupation zone. The cards were in Italian, but contained many obvious words for name, surname, year and place of birth, etc. The only new Italian words on the cards were *salutare* (healthy) and *malati* (sick).

The first echelon of Italians arrived the next day. We sat in ticket booths. When the train arrived, the station became a boiling kettle of noise, songs and joy. I remember these few days as a permanent multi-year concert with songs, dances and festivities. The young, happy and funny boys were returning home. The ticket booth was supposed to service one passenger at a time. The Italians did not know this, or more likely, did not care. At least three funny faces at any time tried to squeeze into the booth simultaneously, pushing each other and generally having a great time. The work was not difficult and we managed it very quickly.

There was a garrison shop where one could buy boots and clothing for just a few pennies. The officer told us that it was very stupid to buy these things, since they would definitely be stolen on our way home. Besides, according to him, there was an abundance of all products, goods and other things for unimaginably low prices in the Soviet Union. We were stupid enough to buy his fairy tales. Freedom and the good life often soften reason and one's internal guard.

As I had learned before, all good things will end. Our work was over and we were put on a train to a new destination: The NKVD Filtration Camp No. 356, Ziertheim. The camp investigators here had unlimited powers. They could send people directly to Siberian camps or back to their homes (with the exception of the so-called sensitive cities, Moscow, Leningrad, Kiev and Sebastopol).

Ziertheim used to be a German tank training base. Dense woods housed huge tank hangars, which had been converted by the

NKVD into dormitories for displaced people. Each hangar had three long rows of four-story bunk beds.

My friend Tolya and I settled on neighboring beds and began waiting to be called by the investigator, in charge of deciding our fate. The overall atmosphere was oppressive. It was dangerous to speak with other prisoners. The lack of information caused frightening rumors to float around. People called for questioning usually returned depressed and could not tell us anything useful. Some never came back.

Three times a day we were led down to the canteen. The food was bearable. Nobody starved. On the way to the canteen we tried not to look at the three-story building which housed the investigators. During meals we did not to talk to each other and pretended that this building served no interest to us.

Finally my day came. The investigator was a young guy about twenty-five years old, wearing a gray suit. His face was plain and his eyes were red and swollen from excessive drinking. I timidly greeted him.

"Tell me!" demanded the investigator.

I could not say even two words before being interrupted by terrible cursing. I got lost for a moment.

"Why are you, you worthless scum, telling me all these fables? Don't you think we know that you collaborated with the Germans and served as a policeman? I have all the incriminating documents right here in front of me!" he screamed.

Blackness covered my eyes and penetrated my heart. I did not know what to do. I thought to tell him my story in great details, but had realized it was pointless. After fifteen minutes of screaming the investigator wrote something on the paper in front of him (it looked like my registration card) and said, "Go and think about it! When you come back I want to hear only the truth!"

I thought I was prepared for every possibility, but after this questioning I was lost. Without any chance to explain myself, I was labeled as a 'Nazi Collaborator' by a semi-drunk investigator and left in complete disgrace. I realized that my four-year captivity had not ended; it had just assumed a different flavor. As they said, I got what I was fighting for.

The next meeting with the investigator never happened. Four days later, all the men of military age were loaded onto trains and sent to the Far East to fight Japan, as was agreed at the Potsdam conference. We were issued food rations for three days.

The rations consisted of six raw potatoes, one kilo of bread and 300 grams of 'sunflower' oil. The 'sunflower' oil smelled and looked like engine oil, which it probably was, except it was so dirty that it was not suitable for lubrication. For a long time afterwards we could not get its smell off of our belongings.

The cars were made out of wood and we had no place to start a fire and bake raw potatoes. But Russian people, who learn to survive under any conditions, quickly found a solution. The train was rather slow and we managed to jump off, pick up bricks, boards and a few sheets of iron on the side of the railway before jumping back onto the moving train. The next day we had a baked potato dinner.

Our destination was the city of Erfurt. I knew that it was located in the state of Thuringia, also called 'The Green Heart of Germany'. I also knew that Johann Sebastian Bach worked somewhere in this area.

At the train station we were met by a lieutenant and a sergeant. We were counted, checked against the list and led to the camp through the quiet and deserted streets. We considered it to be a very good sign that the lieutenant and the soldiers went ahead of the column rather than standing off on the sides, as if guarding prisoners.

After a short march we came to the former German barracks and were given a hot meal. The food was ordinary porridge, but after our experience with raw potatoes and engine oil we thought that we were at a posh restaurant.

At the camp we were told that the Motherland had given us the honor and privilege to be drafted to the Army. After we finished all the paperwork formalities we learned that we had been assigned to a special battalion and would be going to fight Japan. It was hard to describe our happiness that our situation had finally been cleared and we become a part of the Soviet Army. We received our uniforms and went to take a bath. The uniforms were made out of a sandy colored cotton material and were intended for the German expeditionary troops in Africa. The uniforms were extremely comfortable and rather stylish, but we did not like them at all -

someone joked that the reason why our battalion was called 'special' was that it had a German outside with a Soviet inside.

The battalion was based in the city of Neustadt. We lived in very comfortable barracks on the territory of a former factory. The Germans had used these barracks to shelter forced laborers working at the plant. All the plant's equipment had been carefully packed in boxes and prepared for shipment to the Soviet Union.

We lived the usual soldier's life, daily marching, exercises, political lectures, patriotic singing and some Soviet movies in the town's theater. There were few differences from other battalions: we were not issued any weapons and there were frequent questionings by SMERSH, after which some soldiers did not come back. Those who did return were reluctant to tell us anything. The soldiers from other battalions pointed fingers at us and called us 'The Rommel Army'.

One day the commanding officer announced that one of the soldiers had stolen a pig from a German farmer and the military tribunal had sentenced him to death. He asked for volunteers to perform the execution. There were none, and the commander picked five soldiers himself. One of those selected was my friend Tolya. Later he told me the details of the execution.

The soldiers formed a semi-circle on the outskirts of the village. It was a very cold and bleak day. After thirty minutes of waiting the high army commanders arrived in three vehicles. One of the cars brought the German farmers, an elderly couple, against whom the soldier had committed this abominable act. Tolya overheard the farmers begging the officers to spare the soldier because they had voluntarily given him the pig. The officers politely but firmly refused.

Another car brought the accused, a very old and short soldier, wearing a discolored, almost white uniform. With the most pitiful look he walked towards the soldiers without paying any attention to his surroundings and with complete disregard to his fate. One of the officers read his sentence. The soldier was led to a freshly dug pit and his epaulets were torn away. Someone broke out in a heartbreaking cry. It was the farmer's wife who fell to her knees before the officer asking him to pardon the soldier. One officer separated from the group and slowly approached the soldier from behind. He raised his handgun and shot the soldier in the neck.

Recounting the details of this execution Tolya was very distressed. He asked me, "Do you think that the Germans or Americans would shoot one of their soldiers who had fought throughout the entire war for such a minor misconduct?"

"I do not know about other armies, but I would advise you to keep quiet and do not discuss this with anyone," I replied to him.

Our brainwashing continued during the daily boring lectures about the genius of Comrade Stalin, who had led the people to great victory and who brought freedom and prosperity to our country and to the rest of the world. The victory was in fact hard-won, and everyone here knew from their own experience the price we had had to pay for it.

The boring days passed by until the news about Japan's capitulation brought some excitement. I also had my own personal excitement. I was ordered to report to the head of SMERSH. It was impossible to refuse such an invitation. In the words of one of my fellow soldier it was, "Like kissing a tiger; no pleasure and a certainty of being eaten."

Before my appointment I feverishly recalled every conversation I had had with any other soldier, especially if it contained any potentially hazardous jokes. With fear, I reported to the head of SMERSH. I immediately noticed that the major in charge was not young, was definitely sober and did not greet me with cursing. He invited me to sit down and asked about the circumstances of my capture. I told him my story.

"Did you take an oath before the capture?" he asked me.

No, I did not. As a student-volunteer I was assigned to a battalion just a few days before the capture and we never took an oath," I replied.

Our conversation was rather normal but I was on constant guard for the catch. The major was getting closer and closer.

"What kind of talk do you hear in your platoon?"

"Quite ordinary, regular soldier's banter," I responded. "After breakfast we guess what will be for lunch. After each exercise we complain about sore feet and we always talk about women."

Finally, he asked the big question. I realized that this was the reason why he called me in.

"Are you friendly with Anatoly?"

"Yes, has the bed next to mine."

"How did you meet him?"

"We met in the camp right before we came here. For a few days we worked in the local army administration unit helping to register Italian POWs."

"What do you discuss with each other?"

"The same as with everybody else: sports, movies, and the girls we see in the movies."

The interview lasted for about an hour, during most of which he tried to find any information about Tolya. Realizing that I did not know much, he dismissed me and asked to me tell Tolya to immediately report to him.

Anatoly did not return for a long time. When he finally came back, accompanied by the major, his eyes were red and swollen from tears. He asked me for a few cigarettes, gathered his things and left. That was the last I ever saw of him.

I knew Tolya for about a month. I remembered his distress about the execution of the soldier who had taken the pig. He wore his distress on his sleeve that day, walking around with noticeable tears. Despite my warnings, perhaps he had shared his thoughts with someone else and was turned in to the NKVD.

The war with Japan had ended, but it brought back the uncertainty. Dressed in German uniforms and singing Russian patriotic songs we did not know whether we were Soviet soldiers or Soviet prisoners dressed in the enemy's uniforms. The answer to this question was brought home soon enough by the division commander. Before his arrival we went through the typical Soviet Potemkin procedures: cleaning anything visible, fixing everything that looked broken and yelling "Long Live the Comrade General."

All this proved to be unnecessary. The entire battalion gathered in the canteen to meet a very young general wearing a sparkling Order of the Hero of the Soviet Union on his chest. The general told us our destiny. "The Soviet military does not trust you. A lot of former prisoners often defect back to the American zone of occupation. Your battalion is being disbanded and you are to be sent to another NKVD Filtration camp for further investigation."

Whatever may be the proper definition of the word 'distrust', in Soviet reality it could only mean gulags in Siberia. There, I could expect ten years of hard labor and whatever other terrors the Soviet hierarchy might devise.

Everything was done very quickly. They took away our German uniforms, gave us back our old clothes, put us in trucks and sent us back to another Ziertheim filtration facility. The trip by train from Ziertheim to here took two days. The trip on Studebakers back from here to Ziertheim took six hours.

There were several differences between the old and new camps: the old one was No. 356, the new one was No. 254; in the old camp we lived in tank barracks, in the new one we occupied residential barracks, and, most important, the poster affixed to the entrance said "Glory to the Soviet People" while in the in the old one it said "Glory to the Communist Party".

The mood was terrible. The label 'Potential Defector' did not portend anything good. Those especially concerned were former residents of Kiev, Moscow, Leningrad, Sebastopol and a few other cities which were absolutely closed to anyone who had spent even one day in the occupied territory. These people were being sent directly to Siberia or to Ural. I had no illusions about my future.

The investigator was an old man, dressed in civilian clothes. A dim lamp under a green canopy barely illuminated the table. A thin folder was in the middle of the table - obviously it was my case file. Without looking at me, the investigator asked dryly, "Tell me about yourself." Something clicked in my head and I made a very long speech.

"What can I say? Everything I can tell you, I have already told the investigator from Filtration camp No. 356, the SMERSH commander in the Separate Battalion, and have written in my registration card. The only thing that I have never mentioned to anyone before – neither during nor after my captivity - was the fact that I am a Jew. In captivity, if somebody suspected that I was a Jew, I would have been immediately shot. I saw how the Germans dealt with the Jews and with the Communists. It may be irrelevant now, but I just want to tell you all these facts to make sure you have all the details of my biography."

I talked for about twenty-five minutes. The investigator did not interrupt me. He was constantly writing something while I spoke, sometimes casting quick glances at me. I told him that I worried about what had happened to my family, about my two little sisters, that I had only one year left before my college graduation, that I wanted to finish my education to benefit my homeland, and that I had refused job offers from the French and Americans just to be useful to my Motherland as soon as possible.

The investigator stopped writing and sat still for some time, thinking. I finished my confession and watched with painful anticipation. Finally, he sighed, as if making a commitment, and wrote something on the paper.

"You can go now," he said, handing me the paper.

On the way out I read it. It stated "Roman V. Kosovsky passed the background check in the NKVD Filtration Camp No. 254, Ziertheim and is being sent for permanent residence to the city of Kiev, from where he was drafted into the Army." Under the 'Nationality' field of my card was written: 'Jew'.

I turned around and told my investigator, "Thank you very much."

"OK. Go."

The number of people with immense desire to return home had diminished. Apparently, the bulk of displaced people had already gone through 'purgatory' and most were being sent to Siberia and Ural. Our camp was merging with other camps. The only remaining inhabitants here were the former forced laborers.

By late November we started freezing – there was no heat. My feet were reasonably protected – I had well made thick German boots, which I had received in exchange for some of my Herman possessions. These boots loyally served me well up until 1951, when I managed to save enough money to buy my first pair of shoes. A short jacket, given to me by the French, conducted cold and heat equally well and hardly protected me from freezing. The French, ever the trendsetters, had also given me a smart looking vest. Of course, beauty often squashed utility, and this vest had absolutely no insulation function. I picked the cotton from my mattress and stuffed it into the vest to improve its insulation. In this vest I looked like a pregnant woman or a stuffed chicken, depending on who you asked, inviting endless jokes from my neighbors. On top of my designer French chicken vest usually went a rubber raincoat that literally fell apart at the seams in cold weather. With such clothing I would not make it home to Kiev, let alone Siberia.

When the long-awaited day finally arrived, we boarded trucks and the long column of 12 cars started another *'Drang Nach Osten'*. In two days we were set to reach a transit camp near Lvov. We were finally looking at the light at the end of tunnel. So it seemed.

At this point most of us began another stage of our captivity. This time it lasted much longer than the 1307 days spent as a German POW. For me I was to spend nearly ten years as the 'enemy of the people'.

It was freezing in the fast moving open trucks and only the thought of going home kept us warm. The first accident happened within three hours. The third car in our column overturned. We heard heartbreaking cries and saw several people lying motionless on the asphalt. An enraged lieutenant ordered the rest of the truck to continue moving. When asked what had caused a truck to overturn on a dry and straight road, the lieutenant condescendingly retorted, "The driver was a drunken pig."

The road was empty. We passed many gray, abandoned villages. We went through the small towns of Katowitz and Chemnitz in Upper Silesia. This area in 1939 was occupied by Germany and most Poles were expelled or Germanized, like my former boss Alojz Wilczek. Now the opposite was happening - the Poles were returning and there were visible signs of life in the cities, bustle in the factories and smoke from smokestacks.

While still seated in the open trucks, we were met with a hail of stones. The Poles obviously wanted to express their gratitude for their liberation from the Germans and for the large chunk of land that Stalin had taken from Germany and given to Poland. They expressed this deep gratitude to the Russians by stoning our unarmed collection of innocent people and former slave laborers, half of whom were women.

We spent the first night in the school building of a small Polish town. We were allowed to sleep only in the corridors and the lobby. There were no beds or blankets. I took a spot in a corridor near the toilet. When the lieutenant had to go in the middle of the night, he did not hesitate to wake everyone in his way, pushing them aside and yelling, "Get out of the way, rotten intellectuals!"

22. SMOKE OF THE HOMELAND

We arrived at our destination – the township of Gorodok. The weather was terrible with heavy clouds and wet snow. We did not see the town but immediately unloaded and after a roll call were handed over to the NKVD duty officer, who collected all our filtration papers for supposed registration.

A woman led us to the place where we were designated to stay the night. For about ten minutes we were herded across a potato field, finally stopping near potato pits covered with hay. This was our hotel. Men and women were settled into separate potato pits covered with hay. For those who complained about the accommodations the women replied tartly, "Our people in some cities and villages are still living in worse conditions!"

It was probably true, but it did not make our stay any warmer. It was really cold and I fondly remembered my bushlat which had saved me during German captivity. It was so cold that nobody could fall asleep and everyone's brain was on thought overload. Perhaps, it was in such circumstances that man invented fire, boots and coats. Someone quickly figured out to take apart the hay cover of one pit and use it to line the floor of another. This was a good start.

In the morning we learned that armed men had come during the night to the women's huts, raped women and stole belongings.

Some thought that these were soldiers from a nearby garrison. Others felt that the rapists were *Banderas*, Ukrainian nationalist guerillas led by Stephen Bandera, who in the post-war period in Western Ukraine fought the Soviet regime. The night belonged to the *Banderas*, the day to the Communists. To be more precise – there was no order day or night.

We decided to go to the Ministry of Internal Affairs to find out what is going on. A woman who met with us gave the same monotone response to any question we asked.

"When will we get food?"

"I do not know. When they bring it."

"Where is the officer who took our documents?"

"I do not know. He probably went to the administrative office."

"When will we be sent home?"

"I do not know. Probably after the buyers come."

The word 'buyers' ignited my vivid imagination with pictures from history books of slave bazaars, gladiators and galleys. These images fit perfectly into our current situation.

Meanwhile, our persevering hunger forced us to go to the village in attempt to earn some money for food. The village was exceptionally hostile. In some places we were attacked by dogs. In other places we were met by similarly vicious peasants. One peasant did not understand Russian and spoke in a mix of Polish and Ukrainian. When asked about the name of his village he gave the poetic and, as it turned out, quite accurate answer, "Gentlemen, you are in a shithole!"

I translated it to my friend. He looked around and nodded agreeably. The peasant was very talkative and explained that we would not find any work here; nobody was working the fields and nobody was taking care of the farms. There was no authority in the village and everyone was fed up with migrants like us asking for food. The only large city was Lvov, about thirty miles away. With this valuable information we returned to our huts.

The next day was a holiday – the anniversary of the Great October Revolution. We found out about the holiday by the red flag waving proudly on top of city hall and by one half of the slogan: 'Long Live …'. The rest of the slogan was supposed to contain words like 'Stalin', 'Great October Revolution' or 'Communist Party', but the *Banderas* had cut off the other half at night.

Finally we understood that the 'buyers' were recruiters from various defense factories in Siberia and Ural. They were recruiting everyone, irrespective of prior profession or of valid documents. The hunger and freezing weather were extremely convincing recruitment factors. Many realized that they did not have enough food or adequate clothing to survive even a few more days and signed up. I managed to barter my rubber coat for a loaf of bread and decided to wait a little more.

After several days I had no choice but to sign up. I found a suitable buyer - a representative from the Lvov automobile service plant. They needed mechanics, toolmakers, plant operators and a variety of other workers with a high school education. I figured that Lvov was closer to Kiev, so I reasoned there would be no Siberian cold and I could survive in my clothing. Such were the concerns of one with such a tenuous grasp on survival itself.

We were put in a long barracks with a heavy brick wall in the middle. German POWs lived on the other side. Each one of us was issued a personal bed, a towel, and a blanket. After days spent in potato pits without food, my accommodations felt like paradise.

I got a job as an operations planner in the motor shop with a salary of 700 rubles per month plus food vouchers. I learned the job quickly, much faster than milking cows. My technical college education helped a lot. I learned to overhaul many types of engines and began studying the business procedures and operations.

The manager of the shop was Captain Voloshin, a former Kievan. We often reminisced about familiar places and shared common memories. I felt fortunate to have received such a great boss. He treated me well and initially helped me to learn my job.

Once, when remembering pre-war Kiev, Voloshin complained to me, "The Jews are returning to Kiev and our people are being evicted from the apartments where the Jews lived before the war."

What a friend! It was the same old variation on the theme "We fight this war for you", which I had heard years ago. These were quite normal people, not drunks; even the people I knew well and who respected me sometimes would say, "What a good man, shame he is a Jew!"

Nobody mentioned the tragedy of Babi Yar. I wrote a letter to Elizabeth Sakharov, the landlady of the house in Kiev where my aunt had lived, asking her to write me about the fate of my family. Soon I received a big letter from my cousin Fannichka, where she described in sad detail the misfortunes of our family. Of my four male cousins only one returned from the war alive. He lost his right hand. Like me, Fanya's husband was captured and returned home after going through unthinkable trials. My aunt's family settled in the basement where I had lived before the war. This basement was so awful that during or after the war no one even tried to be squatter in them. But at least I had someone in Kiev and I would not be homeless.

I did not get a response to my letters to Chervonoe.

I began to receive food vouchers at work. The food was scarce and, as my co-worker put it, played hide-and-seek with us. It was useless to complain – half of the county was starving. It also was useless to complain that half of the produce intended for us was being stolen before reaching our plates. Such was an honored and inevitable Soviet tradition. One of the Hungarian POWs captured three years before at Stalingrad got fed up with the continuous political brainwashing and invented his own slogan, "A Russian opens his mouth only to lie and pulls his hands out of his pocket only to steal."

I took umbrage. "Nobody invited you here with your Nazi friends. People lived normal lives before you came. You destroyed and pillaged our country and now you have the audacity to criticize!"

I knew that what I said was not true, but I would not take *any* criticism from the enemy. This fellow somehow made certain that I never saw him around the facility again.

The money we earned was useless – the stores were empty. Our standards of living were almost exactly like that of the German POWs. However, unlike the POWs, we were almost free to go out to the city. At the farmers market, in the center of Lvov, we could spend our monthly salary for a half loaf of bread. But our freedom was compromised by the fact that we did not have passports or other documents legitimizing our residency in Lvov.

The city had a curfew. Special police and military units systematically stopped anyone they considered suspicious. Because we did not have proper documents, we were constantly detained and threatened with all kinds of troubles for violating the passport regime. They would release us only after intervention of the Plant Administration.

Lvov had had an equal population of Poles, Ukrainians and Jews before the war. The Jews were exterminated by the Germans with the enthusiastic cooperation of the Poles and Ukrainians. Now the Poles living in the city were selling their houses for nothing and were moving to Poland. They were in a rush. After a few years, the Polish population of Lvov had diminished to less than one percent. Some plant employees were able to buy comfortable mansions and furniture for a pittance.

We decided to send someone to the Ministry of Internal Affairs, to check on the documents that had taken from us. The delegate returned by the end of the day.

First he ran to me screaming, "Roman – you owe us a bottle of vodka and a dance!"

It turned out that the department of the Ministry of Internal Affairs, which had taken our documents, no longer existed. An old lady, presumably a night custodian in the building where this department was located, was using a big pile of documents to heat the furnace. These documents were priceless certifications and permits to live in particular cities, issued by the Filtration Camp investigation. By miracle, my documents were the only ones to survive. How could it be that I was so lucky? I read my paper countless times and could not believe my incredulous eyes, "Kosovsky, Roman Vladimirovich has passed the background test in the Filtration camp and is being sent by the Ministry of Internal Affairs for permanent residence to the city of Kiev." This was a dream come true, a magic 'get out of jail' card, a permit for a normal life.

Suddenly I remembered. Had my co-workers seen what was written in the Nationality box? Did they find out that I was a Jew? For almost four years I had carefully concealed my nationality and I was not sure how my comrades would accept this news. I looked at their faces, but they just pat me on my back, congratulated me and demanded a bottle.

The sense of anxiety about someone finding out that I was a Jew stayed with me for thirty-five more years until I left the Soviet Union. Initially I thought that it was a consequence of my captivity, but recently I realized that this is common among all persecuted people, in particular the Jews of the Soviet Union. I watched an interview of one very famous artist who recounted how in the Soviet Union, before he entered a bus, subway or other public place, he unconsciously would assess the situation for any potential danger. Only after arrival in Israel did he lose this habit. I got chills listening to how exactly this man's feelings of constant insecurity mirrored my own.

Naturally, I was very pleased to comply with the people's will and got the vodka. To do so I had to visit an establishment run by one 'aunt Maria' located about 100 yards from the plant. For a modest price, Maria supplied the whole factory with incredibly awful and smelly moonshine. This place was very popular and the workers made a special passage in the perimeter fence to make sure that supplies were accessible during curfew. Once I fulfilled my moonshine duties I began to think about how I would obtain a passport and become a real citizen. They used to say in the Soviet Union, "Without papers you are shit; with papers you are a man."

At first, I made an appointment with the Plant Director. I showed him my paper and asked for a two week vacation in order to go to Kiev and obtain a passport (in the Soviet Union passports were the main IDs and were issued exclusively by the place where one was assigned to live). The Plant Director, who also was a

Colonel, refused – he was short on workers and a few of them had not returned after vacations.

I could not leave my workplace without permission. It was a criminal offense in the Soviet Union, punishable by three years of hard labor in the camps. It was in this Communist Serfdom that we were fed patriotic songs, like *I don't know any other country in the world where a person can breathe so free!*

I decided to go with the less risky option. Next time I was stopped on the street for a curfew violation I showed my papers and asked to be issued a passport. They refused. I had been sent to Kiev so therefore they could not issue me a passport in Lvov.

"What should I do?" I asked.

"You can do whatever you want, but if we catch you next time you will go to jail for passport regime violation."

In past centuries, during the times of serfdom, Russia had one special day of the year, called 'Yuri's Day', during which a serf was allowed to leave his master and go to another. I desperately had to find my own 'Yuri's Day'.

Suddenly, it dawned on me how to get out. I said to the officer, "You will not issue me the passport. You will not recognize my papers issued by the Filtration Camp as basis for me to stay in Lvov! In that case you have to write me an order to leave Lvov within forty-eight hours!"

And another unexpected thing happened - the officer issued me an order to leave Lvov within twenty-four hours. Two papers (the original document from the filtration camp and just issued order) were sufficient to obtain the third one next day– a rail ticket to Kiev[25].

---

[25] For someone who never lived in Soviet Union, especially during Stalin's time it is impossible to comprehend the myriad or regulations and restrictions governing day to day life. Passport was the most important document, subject to verification at any moment, without which a person could not travel inside the country (nobody could travel outside the country). People without passports (including most peasants) were not allowed to live in the cities and could be arrested on the spot. Special permits and orders were needed to change jobs, move to another address, etc. Having at least two supporting documents was necessary to restore the one which was lost.

23. IN KIEV

I will never forget the gray day of March 5th, 1946. The skies were gray, the dilapidated buildings were gray, the shadows of people on the streets were gray, and the whole city was gray. I was walking through the city anticipating the joy of meeting my family.

The meeting was joyous; the stories of the losses were sad. I started a new stage in my life. I was no longer a prisoner, but for another long five years the label of 'traitor' was firmly attached to me, along with millions of prisoners of war and laborers forcibly taken to Germany, who were lucky enough not be sent to the Siberian camps on their return.

First, I took back my name, Rafail. Second, I started indicating my true nationality – a Jew, in all questionnaires and applications. Four professors from my college helped me to restore my education credits. A few good people helped me to find a job.

However, it looked as if there were no good people in the Police. Every three to six months I had to endure another round of questioning and get a temporary certificate of residence in Kiev. In September 1949, my luck ended. After being interrogated by some Major of the Police Force I was told that Kiev was overpopulated and I had seventy-two hours to leave the city.

Either from anger or from despair, I wrote a very politically dangerous letter to the chief of Passport Control. I had nothing to lose and figured that they would not send me back to Germany and if they decided to send me somewhere else, at least they would pay for it.

When I was called to the Passport Control office, I took all my belongings with me just in case – I was sure I would be arrested. I met the Colonel of the Police Force. He listened to my explanations and told me to wait in the reception. After a short while, he called into his office the Major who had previously ordered me to leave Kiev in seventy-two hours. For about a quarter of an hour I heard heavy cursing from the Colonel's cabinet, after which the Major appeared and angrily said to me, "Why would you not tell me everything the last time I saw you?" and left.

A few days later I received an official notice that I was to be granted a permanent residence in Kiev. Thus, I learned that sometimes good people could be found even in the Police Force ranks. I came to the police station to fill out my passport application.

An elderly police clerk looked at my form then looked at me curiously and asked, "What do you want me to put in the Nationality field?"

"A Jew," I replied. "This is what I wrote in the application."

"Are you sure? Did you think hard enough?" she asked.

"Yes," I replied. "My entire family was Jewish and I want to be like them. To do otherwise would mean to betray their memory."

In a country where a full-born antisemitic campaign had just started, this good woman tried to forewarn and help me.

24. POST SCRIPTUM

I finally got my full "freedom" (the word freedom is not the best to describe my situation). At exactly the same time an ugly antisemitic propaganda campaign had been initiated by the Communist Party. It fell on the fertile ground of traditional Russian and Ukrainian antisemitism heated by German Nazism. Soviet Communism and German Nazism become hardly distinguishable from each other. By 1952, the antisemitic campaign reached its apogee and trains were ready to forcibly evacuate the entire Jewish population to Siberia. Only the death of Stalin interrupted these plans and prevented another final solution. Official antisemitism never fully ceased. It was incredibly difficult for Jewish kids to be accepted into college, receive a good job or advance their careers. Still, despite all adversities, all my Jewish friends' children managed to study hard, get an education and become top-notch professionals.

At the same time I fully absorbed Russian culture. The language, songs, books, and poetry had become my second nature, my 'software'. I don't see any contradictions in this duality. Later I immersed myself into American culture, both difficult because of my older age and simultaneously easy because I found its basic principles to be fully in sync with my core beliefs.

I have often asked myself whether I did the right thing when I returned to the Soviet Union. I still don't have the answer. I could not stay in the cesspool into which the Nazis had turned Germany. But when I returned, I realized that I arrived in the Soviet version of the same cesspool. I finally understood that the Communism in which I believed does not and could not exist.

Free or in captivity, I always feel that I am a Jew. I have forgotten the prayers my father taught me. I have forgotten the Hebrew alphabet and I consider myself a secular Jew, but every time I step into a synagogue, I feel a strange excitement. I feel that I am getting in touch with something holy and getting closer to some profound age-old secret.

It might be obvious for any reader of these memoirs that the dominant theme of my life story is antisemitism. I have given this phenomenon a great deal of thought, trying to understand why the Jews, who as a people have made such a great contribution to humanity, have so many haters. I see basic human and political components to this phenomenon. Perhaps the word "human" is more of a euphemism for what is in fact an ugly manifestation of basic zoological instincts.

For thousands of years the Jews led distinct religious and secular lives with special emphasis on education, hard work and making the best living under any circumstances. This always caused envy, resentment and anger from their neighbors. If such inherently negative feelings are not moderated by education, the cultural environment, and the political system, tragedy is almost inevitable.

I understood the political side of this issue by reading an article by Shulgin - the former Chairman of the Russian State Duma during the early 20th century. He was a vivid monarchist and antisemite. I stumbled on his brochure appropriately titled "Why we don't like you." In this small booklet he accuses the Jews of insufficient patriotism, resistance of assimilation and many other sins, and in conclusion he finds that after two thousand years of Jewish experience in economy, trade, and the sciences, the Russian Jew possesses superior qualifications and therefore the State must limit their activities in favor of Russian businessmen. This is, so to speak, the political component of anti-Semitism.

But all of this has no direct relationship to my story. Regardless of political systems, regardless of basic human nature, in the most of the difficult situations I was fortunate enough to meet good people willing to help me and save me. This is what brings happiness to me – the knowledge that the world is not without good people and that good people are in the majority.

It just seems like that the good is always less noticeable than the evil.

www.ingramcontent.com/pod-product-compliance
Lightning Source LLC
LaVergne TN
LVHW011223080426
835509LV00005B/285